EQUESTRIAN SPORT:
SECRETS OF THE "ART"
AN ANTHOLOGY

Edited by

LYDIA NEVZOROVA

Equestrian Sport: Secrets of the "Art"

Copyright © 2012 Nevzorov Haute École

Photographs © Lydia Nevzorova, Sophia Spartantseva, Natalya Bykova, Georgi Gavrilenko, Anastasia Grogorieva, Anastasia Nekrasova, Catherine Scott

Photos on pages 92, 102 provided by Sophia Spartantseva, photos on pages 4, 26, 30, 46 provided by Georgi Gavrilenko, photo on page 68 provided by Lydia Nevzorova, photo on page 124 provided by Catherine Scott, illustration on page 55 provided by Sumereshnaya.

Published by Nevzorov Haute École

www.hauteecole.ru

ISBN 978-5-904788-18-6

Project Head: Lydia Nevzorova

Managing Editor: Donna Condrey-Miller

Editor: Stasya Zolotova

Editorial Staff: Varvara Lyubovnaya, Cloé Lacroix, Marie Duizidou

Art Director: Dmitri Raikin

Head of Pre-press Department: Eugene Mushtay

Cover Photo: Sophia Spartantseva

CONTENTS

NEUROCRANIALIS SHOCK

It is clear, that not a single regular or accidental reader of this book will get as low as doing ES (equestrian sports). Nevertheless it seems to me that some profound and adequate analysis of the base facts is absolutely necessary for one to get a general education in hippology.

While this phenomenon still exists it is necessary to gain the understanding of it.

It is already well known that ES is extremely unnatural, torturous and disastrous for any horse.

But competitions of different levels and Olympiads are still taking place.

And it's not just people who are taking part in it, but horses too.

It's clear that participation of horses in it all is because they are forced, they don't volunteer. It's clear that the iron tools fixed in their mouths are a frightful argument designed for torturing and killing a horse, compelling enough to make any horse obey even an ape that is sitting on its back.

The bit.

A barbaric invention of the bronze century, yet still being used in spite of the fact that veterinary science has already passed its verdict against it.

But we don't want to limit our explanations just to the term "horse bits" or "bit". What we need is serious and qualitative analysis, separate and apart from its use.

So-called selfish pleasure seekers or jockeys of all trades, as well as sportsmen, make all imaginable efforts to justify the use of bits. Taking their opinion into account on this matter is senseless, as their motivation is obvious.

The point is that exact and perfect scientific knowledge of the use of the bit and its impact is, alas, an integral part of the history of hippology. No doubt, its application is shameful and neolithic, but it doesn't mean that we should be ignorant about techniques of its application. Horse and man's interactions

Photo 1. © Georgi Gavrilenko

Photo 2. © Georgi Gavrilenko

have been based on these techniques for a very long time now. That is why the relationship has transformed into such an ugly form.

We know that being controlled by horror, pain, fear of pain and beating, horses are jumping over painted bars (show-jumping) or demonstrating reflexive, marionette like painful movements (dressage), only for the fun of the audience. And they don't do it just once or twice.

Let's leave it to amateurs and absolute idiots to tell stories about horses, which perform those actions that are considered normal in sports at their own will. It is imbecilic bullshit which contradicts the physiology, anatomy and psychology of a horse, and cannot be taken seriously.

But the term "bit" is not an answer to all questions in spite of its terrible implication for any horse. If it was all about the bit, this instrument would easily enable everyone involved in this sport to become Olympic champions. Amateur and professional horse riders put the iron tool of identical configuration, with identical strength and impact of pain into the horse's mouth. And nevertheless not all riders become champions. The majority (99 percent) of so-called riders demonstrate ridiculous or better to say, shameful, failures (even according to their own sport norms and requirements) and look ridiculous.

So what's the secret? How do some riders force the horse to perform these completely senseless and extremely painful actions? Are there any special tricks or basic methods that work which have been developed and thoroughly tested? Does their "correct" application guarantee the success in the ES business?

Such a set of methods does exist. ES success lies ONLY in mastering these methods, their constant improvement, and in extremely ruthless application of them. Taking into account that all these tricks cause unbearable pain effects on the mouth, the neurological system of the head, and destroy the whole physiological and anatomic system of the horse, every rider has to have an appropriate level of "deafness" to the horse's sufferings. The man who is capable of feeling what a horse feels would simply go insane if he felt the effect of these tricks just once in his life. There is no exaggeration here. One should remember that there were people servicing fascist gas chambers and they indeed found pleasure in doing so. But others committed suicide or went crazy afterwards.

It is a well known fact that people have different sorts of inclinations.

Even a quick look at "successful" riders proves that alongside their inherited pathological cruelty to the horse, very low I.Q. is also a necessary attribute of "success" in ES.

Low I.Q. guarantees the lack of interest in physiology, anatomy and the history of relationships of people with horses. And it's because interest inspires thirst for knowledge, knowledge will bring along understanding and understanding may provoke sympathy to a horse — and then they will have to say farewell to the "painted bars" and "big prizes".

The most curious thing is that riders deny the existence of these primitive tricks designed to inflict pain, and mumble something about "respect", "contact", "mutual understanding", "soft hands" and things of that nature.

All are typical lies.

Sometimes it's conscious, sometimes it's the result of unbelievable ignorance. By the way, the second version is a more common one. Only absolutely "vampiric masters" know the real truth. But more often they just understand this severe correlation "pain = success" better than others. But there are some others who are well aware of what's going on. We will talk about these "others" later. In fact, everything is rather primitive. Riders have to know how to create a hellish amount of pain so high that it deprives a horse from any choice.

But one has to do it skillfully. For this purpose they have worked out the techniques that we are going to disassemble and analyze. Nowadays, when a huge database of photo and video evidence has been created and numerous examinations and scientific research have been carried out, it's possible to prove the existence of these primitive and painful methods which are the foundation of ES — and show them to a wide audience.

The main task was to identify COMPLETELY IDENTICAL actions that cause absolute pain due to their nature. These are performed by sportsmen of different levels and ages. The task required photo and video materials that would prove that a young pony rider in a provincial sport school and adult winners of honorable championships of Russia, do absolutely identical things. It sounds terrible, but this treatment of horses meets "formal requirements" or is in accordance to the standards. These images give us the right to speak about the systematic approach of torture that is used on horses in ES. It should be emphasized that tearing their mouths, DELIBERATELY causing sharp damaging pressure on their teeth, soft tissues of the mouth, on the entire nervous system of the head are not abuses done by an individual rider or just an unlucky moment.

All masks are off.

Even a quick glimpse of the photo material is enough to see the system. We can see clearly how different people at different ages and different riding levels

Photo 3. © Georgi Gavrilenko

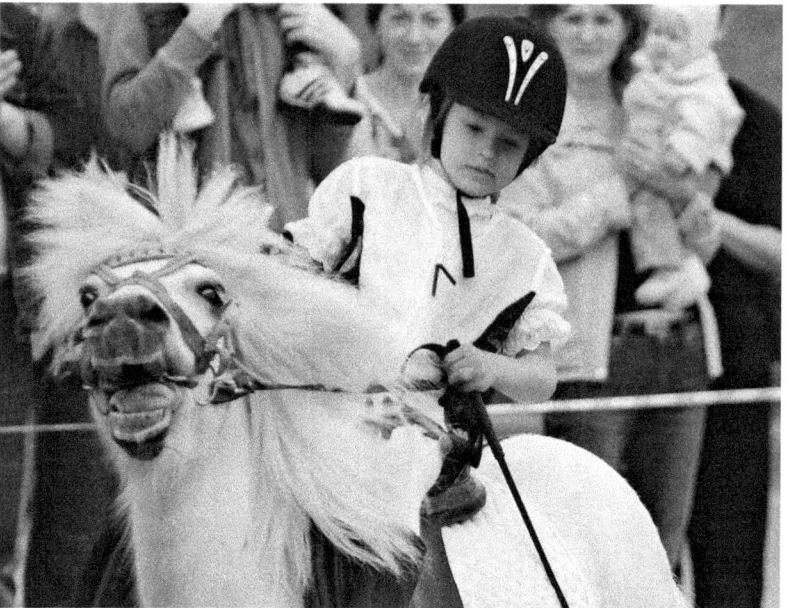

Photo 4. © Georgi Gavrilenko

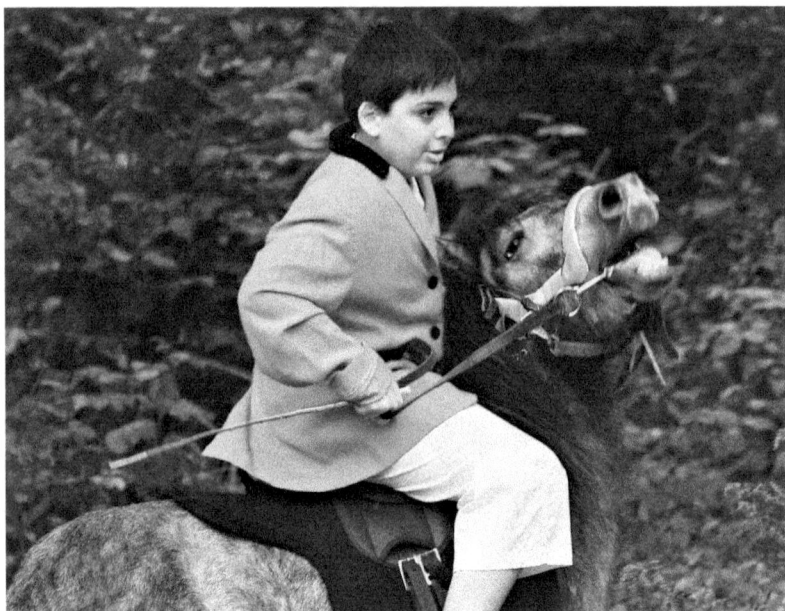

Photo 5. © Nevzorov Haute École

Photo 6. © Georgi Gavrilenko

repeat the same movements, the same techniques, and do it deliberately, and precisely. We have an indisputable right to emphasize that these inflictions or, better to say, tortures can be compared only with a strong electric shock as for their effect on the head's nervous system. Please note that these techniques are considered to be OBLIGATORY elements of horse control in ES.

Up until now, no one has created a convincing, STRICTLY DOCUMENTARY register of methods that are in wide use in ES. A part of this unique register is in front of you. The actual one includes so many photographs it is impossible to present all of them here.

Now, Methods N.1 and N.2

For verbal clarification of the actions that are presented in convincing photographic evidence in this chapter, representing the primary techniques that enable the obedience of a horse in ES; these are considered to be common practice by all criteria and are most appropriately called "NEUROCRANIALIS SHOCK (shock of the nervous system of the skull). This term is highly correct and very informed.

There is only one difficulty, to denote or somehow verbally label the physiological difference between the above methods. In principle there is no physiological difference at all in the application of the first or second method.

But!

The methods have external, visual differences in their execution. In the use of method (let's call it) N.1, we see a very rigid rein grab by one hand and a very strong pull by the other hand, which is so powerful that half of the bit rushes through the horse's mouth, and the rider's elbow goes back as far as possible. This sharp elbow movement increases the leverage force of the bit accordingly, and results in an especially severe and painful blow to the left or right part of horse's skull.

Method N.2 represents an even sharper direct blow by the bit, over all the sensitive areas of horse's mouth. As a rule, every horse who has been forced this way, tries to weaken the effect of the blow by tossing its head up.

The purpose of both methods considered above, that are the basic methods of ES, is to "inflame" the entire innervational system of skull (namely, all the sensitive and complex network of nerves from 12 pairs of head nerves) by a sharp painful impact.

AUTOPSY # 37. (DISSECTION DEPARTAMENT – NERVI CRANIALIS)

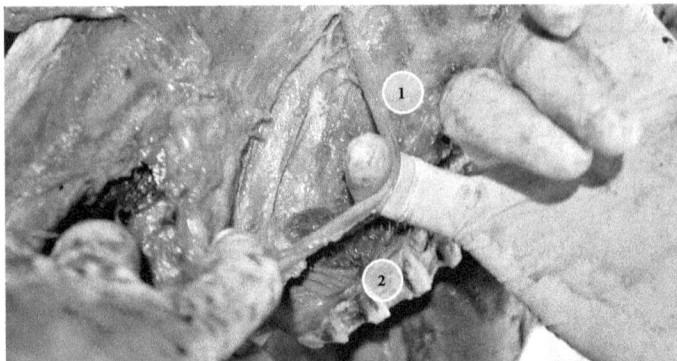

Table A. Points of impact from bit action. Demonstration of the nerves of the skull
1 — n. facialis; 2 — dentes premolars

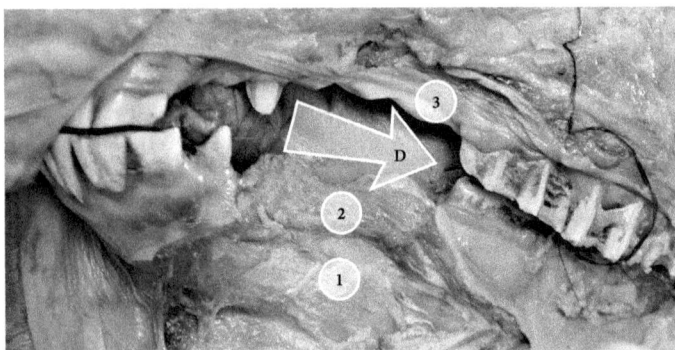

Table B. Points of impact from bit action. Demonstration of the nerves of the skull
1 — n. trigeminus; 2 — margo interalveolaris; 3 — palatum molle

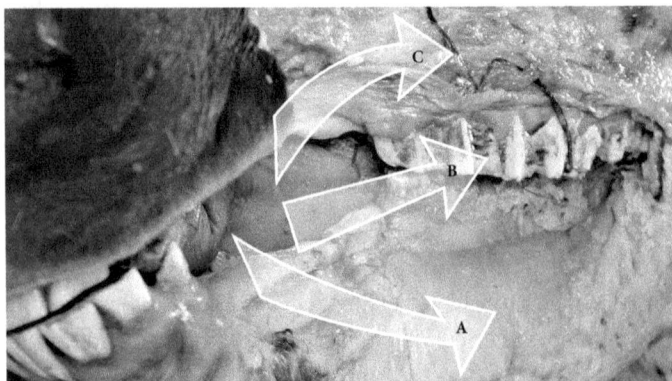

Table C. Points of impact from bit action. Demonstration of the nerves of the skull
n. trigeminus; margo interalveolaris; palatum molle; dentes premolars
A — The first impact direction; **B** — The second impact direction; **C** — The third impact direction; **D** — fourth impact direction (see Table B. above)

Considering the proximity and direct routing of the cranial nerves to the brain, the shock effect is achieved instantly.

Official data from research carried out by the scientific department of Nevzorov Haute École together with JMRC (St.-Petersburg Judicial Medical Research Centre) prove that bit pressure on soft tissues of the mouth and teeth reaches 300 kg per sq.cm when a typical pull/jerk action is used. (see Appendix 2, page 141)

It is a fact that is confirmed by scientific research protocols and expertise. Even if the pull/jerk was five times less it would still inevitably cause the most severe pain, and even at three times weaker, its effect on any living tissues would still be equal to ruthless pain shock.

That is also a scientific fact confirmed by the following series of experiments.

What's relevant is that neither age nor physical condition of the rider can be taken into consideration. The leverage system of reins and the design of the bit enable everyone, from a 13-year old boy to a 23-year old girl or even a 43-year old adult (control group), to achieve practically identical effects and identical force.

Certainly, there is a slight difference, but it's not significant. It mainly depends on age and force of the person using these methods and varies within 20 to 25 kg per sq cm with a jerk action, and within 5 to 8 kg with a standard rein stretch. To summarize, jerks of the first and second type of technique have been thoroughly tested and gave the most stunning results (300 kg per sq cm of a horse's mouth) and they are the ones which are the most frequently and widely used in ES.

What we can see in the photos are these techniques being used, and so we can speak with confidence about the powerful effect they have on soft tissues, skull bones, teeth and nerves.

These training methods turn out to be very effective and are used EVERYWHERE. Each sportsman applies these methods from five to 30 times during each training session or competition (it's confirmed by video and photo documents[1]).

---

[1] These photos were taken at five competitions and two open training sessions. We investigated the actions of some international level sport masters, journeyman of sports, candidates for the journeyman of sports and amateurs.

Not a single horse can oppose any of these methods. A horse is absolutely defenseless in this case.

Moreover, these techniques have been carefully perfected. Skillful application of neurocranialis shock makes champions out of some riders. However, it is used by EVERY SINGLE person practicing ES or pleasure riding. The first things that every child is taught, when joining any riding school, are these methods.

You can make sure of that with the photo 4.

Our next task is to analyze photo documents calmly, just like we do it every day, and translate those actions that have been fixed by the camera into the language of physiology and neurology. So let's go ahead and give them our full attention with all possible precision.

First, let's consider the following situation: resistance of a horse, its unwillingness to perform unnecessary and painful actions. A horse by its nature is absolutely physiological. This means that its attitude to the world rests primarily on its physiological sensations.

Everything connected with training is painful in its essence and we won't discuss it as it has already been uncovered in a number of my articles.

In order to force a horse to do a number of simple actions required by a rider, causing a horse physical pain of average level — having the effect of a bit in its mouth is quite enough in order to "control" it.

Pain and discomfort caused by rein pressure are always sharper and more extreme than pain in its back, neck or legs. A horse will obey this pain and a person who causes it. But doing more complicated actions provokes serious resistance because these actions come in conflict with the myological and physiological nature of a horse.

And at this very moment the rider inflicts a blow with the bit resulting in neurocranialis shock, resulting in pain that considerably surpasses any discomfort or any negative or painful feelings from a high jump over painted bars or any dressage element. As you see, it's all very simple. The rider has one task — execute a skillful blow at the very right moment. In spite of the apparent simplicity of this method only a few riders can master it perfectly; these few are associated with ES ratings. As I've already mentioned, successful application of these methods requires a number of very specific personal qualities. Failure-riders, amateurs and selfish pleasure seekers also use these methods in exactly the same way. They use them on a regular basis and without much skill, thus provoking open rebellion with the subsequent fall of a rider.

An awkward bit strike does not cancel neurocranialis shock, but when it is used improperly it can lead to unpredictable and undesirable consequences rather than those desired.

There is also one curious detail — so called "instant blindness". No serious studies on this topic have been carried out so far, so we can't take it as hippologically scientific, but in a human being, as a result of the same neurocranialis shock, blindness is instant. This partial or complete loss of sight doesn't last long. Its origin and mechanism have been investigated and described (for humans).

It is very likely that a horse that has been subjected to the state of neurocranialis shock too early or too late when coming to the jump is unable to evaluate its height, so it causes so called "collapses".

I emphasize that this statement has no supportable scientific background and is an assumption.

Lets move to proven and obvious facts. It would be incorrect to declare that the base of ES is in pain shock application as some sort of new discovery in hippology. Aside from works and studies done by professors R.Cook, P. Mc-Greevy, A. Warren, S.Skinner and others, there are also quite a number of mature works that are credible, by Russian scientists, that obviously describe practices like that. Even such a scholar as professor A. Laskov [2] talks openly about the "great destructive effect of bits on the mouth cavity of a horse" and also about its effect on the horse's neurological system, and finally about blows inflicted by the bit (page 107–108) in his study "Horse training for the Olympic equine sports" (RSRIH, Russian scientific research institute of horse-keeping, 1997). He writes that the horse has "an extremely sensitive mouth surface" (page 79).

A. Laskov is being honest: "Pain irritators instantly turn on general starting mechanisms of protectively-adaptive reactions in a nervous-reflectory way".

---

[2] Laskov is a veterinarian, biologist and an international category trainer. He was a veterinarian of the ES team in the former USSR, chief manager of the complex scientific group on ES and director of RSRIH laboratory.

Dr. Laskov identifies that "even short term pain irritations considerably change the reflective activity of its [a horse's] spinalcord brain, and condition-reflex the large hemisphere activity."

With the reference to symptoms, what is described here is neurocranialis shock in its essence.

Nevertheless, we've got to make a reservation.

Professor A. Laskov AGREES TO the use of these powerful pain irritators and does it easily. He is extremely honest about this point: "Strong pain irritators should not be used on a day to day basis or as a regular technique in order to make a horse jump. IT CAN BE APPLIED but only in the case of developing or perfecting conditional reflexes of a horse." (p. 152)

What this means is that ES veterinary is well aware of the neurocranialis shock, it finds it acceptable and allows its application. The same person, Laskov, also describes the typical behavior of a horse during the competitions and again he is very honest about it: "Before a jump its breathing gets intense, more frequent, and more shallow than usual. Judging by those symptoms, it mirrors identical breathing patterns exhibited at moments when the entire nervous system anticipates action resulting in severe pain" (Page 152–153). And so on.

You may come across this kind of evidence looking through studies by RSRIH scientists at almost every step. If you open any level of project just at random, for example work by Ms. Parisheva (RSRIH, 1987): "The role of correlation between motional respiratory and heart rhythms of fast gaited horses" — you will find there a detailed and careful analysis of regular and extremely powerful pain irritators and their effect, and complete recognition of their use in ES practices. She provides some sufficient proof of their provocative effect resulting in general physiological stress and pathological destruction of functional heart activity. (Page 114, 118, 121, 122.)

The frankness of these ES ideologists seems shockingly paradoxical, but one should bear in mind that this research was done and published in the 1980's and 90's, before ours, when there was no one and nothing to be ashamed by ES. But nowadays, these statements look like ruthless self-exposure. During those days no one would have thought that these studies would be turned against ES.

Photo 7. © Anastasia Grigorieva

Photo 8. © Georgi Gavrilenko

Photo 9. © Georgi Gavrilenko

Photo 10. © Georgi Gavrilenko

Photo 11. © Sophia Spartantseva

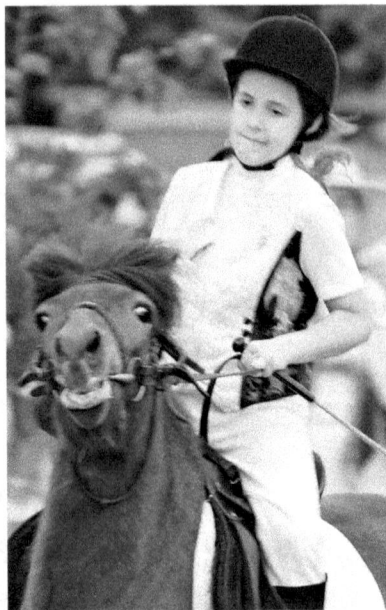
Photo 12. © Georgi Gavrilenko

Consequences of the blow produced by a bit can be defined as neurocranialis shock, without any doubt, judging by the symptoms which were so kindly provided by Mr. Laskov, who had systematized and formulated them with other hot-shots of RSRIH into graphs and tables.

These graphs and tables from the *Military-field Veterinary Guides* textbook are referred to as the only source of information, because nobody else had studied the traumatic shock in horses

(*Military-field Veterinary Guides*. Timofeev, K. Malcev. — M, 2003).

Let's look at the second chapter, part N. 3, page 24: "The mechanical pressure on the nervous system — as an etiological factor of the traumatic shock.

Pathogeneses of traumatic shock is complicated. It can be explained as follows: it's a mechanical trauma caused by painful irritation combined with extreme alertness and excitation of the brain's core.

Then comes the surprising evidence disclosing the extremes in the horse's behavior on the show-jumping field: "We can point out two phases in the traumatic shock. The first (or erectile) phase follows the mechanical trauma. It is usually short and is characterized by a very strong excitation."

Look at page 184, the section called "latent damages of skull and brain" (as a result of pain shock in the head) where pathological-anatomy data is provided: "Sharp filling of soft tissues with venous blood, their swelling (often unevenly) and numerous small hemorrhages." These facts have striking coincidence with the results of the pathological-anatomy data that is describing the "sport" horse's brain condition. So, the fact that ES is based on the hell-like torture remains an unknown only for absolutely ignorant laymen. But we are going off our main topic.

Let's consider the technique of striking a neurocranialis shock blow. As it is clearly seen from all the photos without exception, this kind of blow instantly injures practically all of the cranial (skull) network of nerves.

Tables 1 and 2 show exactly where the bit blows while performing these techniques. We need to learn about "target areas" which are damaged.

The first area is teeth, or to be more exact – the second premolars of the lower jaw (dentes premolars II). It should be stressed that with skillful

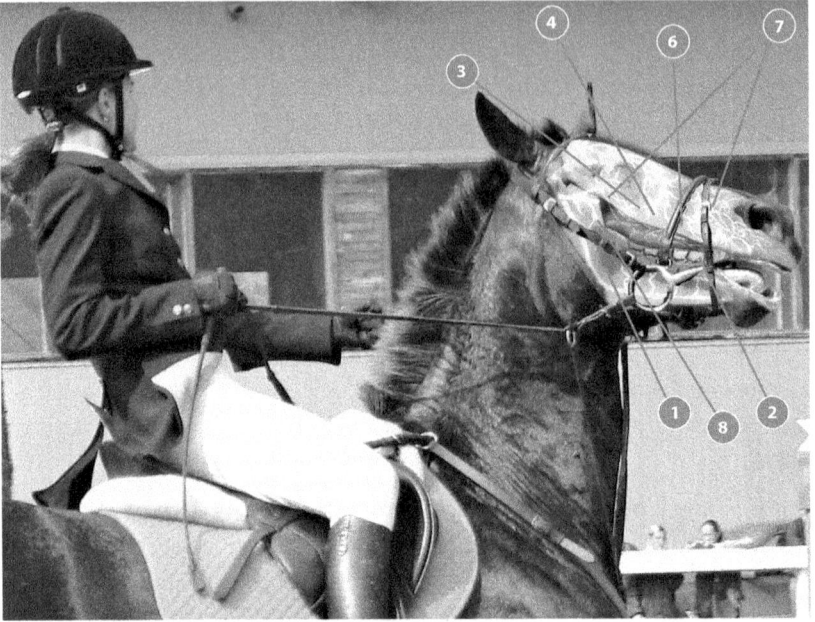

Table 1

Table 2

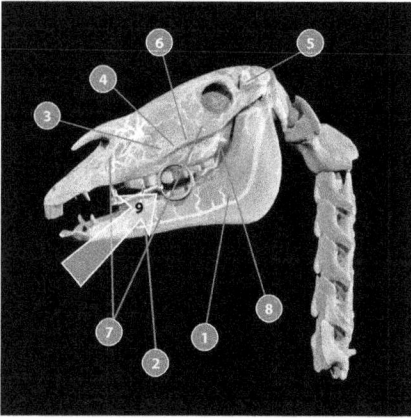

Table 3

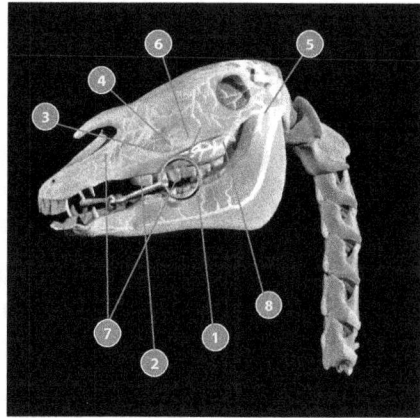

Table 4

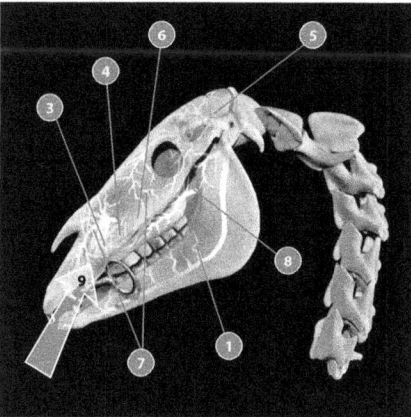

Table 5

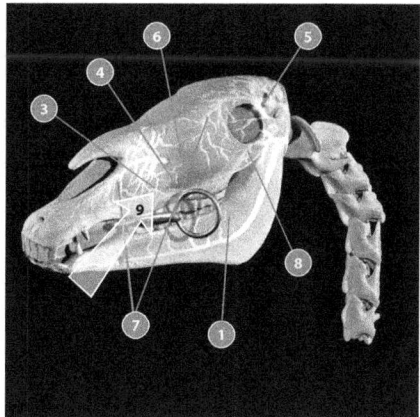

Table 6

DIAGRAM EXPLANATION

1 — Trigeminal nerve branching (*n. trigeminus*); **2** — Second premolars (*dentes premolars II*);
3 — Facial nerve (*n. facialis*); **4** — Lingual nerve (*n. lingualis*); **5** — Brain (*encephalon*);
6 — Small palate nerve (*n. palatinus minor*); **7** — Infraorbital nerve (*n. infraorbitalis*);
8 — Mandibular alveolar nerve (*n. alveolaris mandibulae*);
9 — The impact of the bit.

application of these techniques, the area of damage is exactly the second premolars of the lower jaw.

Without skillful application — upper jaw (see scheme on page 12 and schemes on pages 20–21).

All the photos capture the depth of the bit penetration very clearly, and Tables 1 and 2 convincingly demonstrate the bit blow direction.

The blow injures the under-eye nerve (n. infraorbitalis), which leads to painful detonation of the whole upper part of the skull's nervous system (Table 6).

The second "object of damage" is diastemas (margo interalveolaris). A powerful blow of 300 kg per centimeter strikes the main exit from the foramen into the subsequent dense branch of the trigeminal nerve — (n. trigeminal, Table C).

It "fires up" the lower cranial nervous branch which locks directly on the brain (see Table 4).

The third direction of the pain blow is to the lingual (n. lingualis) nerve and all its peripheral branches. Photos 3, 5, 6, 7 illustrate its disastrous effect — the degree of the bit's effect on the tongue.

The lingual nerve (supersensitive and excessively conductive) fires up the complex and dense system of facial nerves — n. facialis (Tables B and 5) that have reversible connections with it. Pain shock seems to reach its peak. But at this very moment one more horrible factor comes into action. You see, the soft palate (vellum palatinum) of a horse has a very specific structure. It is very long and goes down slantwise, decreasing the palatal arch. Right there, into this very low upper soft palate, supplied with very sensitive palate nerves (n. palatines minor) directly locked on the brain, the violent blow of the bit joint arrives.

See photos 2, 10.

As a result we get a large scale pain climax in the horse's skull, — neurocranialis shock — the foundation of ES. I'd like to stress that we don't speak about the extremes, but about every day practice, about the most common techniques taught in ES with only one purpose — to force a horse to perform various maneuvers. As you can see, a horse has no choice left: painful, blinding, deafening shock or painted bars. And this living hell is every day ES reality.

Let's take a very striking recent fact. I have chosen this fact deliberately, as it is fresh and well known, although there are a lot of others similar examples.

Photo 13. © Georgi Gavrilenko

Photo 14. © Georgi Gavrilenko

Regular Horse Racing. Bay Meadows Racetrack in California. Top jockey Russell Baze takes off on horse called Imperial Eyes. The horse stumbled and all of a sudden "loses" speed. By means of the bit and a whip the jockey makes it gallop further and further and get to the finish line. In a few minutes vets stated there was a severe fracture of a front leg. Video recording made it possible to spot the exact moment of fracture. It was clear that the fracture took place at the moment when the horse presumably "stumbled".

Now it is obvious that Imperial Eyes was galloping with a broken front leg up to the finish line. The horse, of course, was then murdered.

Maybe my review of these events is somewhat impersonal or casual, but similar races are held everywhere, it is common practice.

Its not that. The pain from a front leg fracture is unbearable, it's clear. How strong the bit blow must be to make horse obey under the circumstances. Not only obey but gallop with a broken leg? It must exceed the pain from a fracture. This pain must have been not only extreme but physiologically more dangerous. Pain in the skull is perceived as more threatening and can be compared with the extreme explosion that is injuring the central nervous system and brain, namely this type of a pain is created during the neurocranialis blow. In horse racing neurocranialis shock is applied with the same frequency as in all kinds of ES (photo 11).

Photo documents have been selected so as to illustrate the actions of riders at every so-called level — from the prizewinners at the Russian championships to the amateur horse riders.

Method N. 2, as mentioned above, doesn't vary from method N.1 in its essence. The scheme is approximately the same and neurocranialis shock is achieved in the same way. However, there is a slight difference, due to equal and bilateral bit blow- it penetrates up to the third premolars (dentes premolars III), and affects both upper and lower radical teeth and thepain shock, probably, is more intensive than that achieved with method N. 1.

A much deeper penetration of the bit into the mouth cavity, a larger and steeper force of blow affecting the tongue and tongue nerve is well illustrated with photos 3, 5, 6–7, 14. Thus, it is possible to speak about the two major methods in ES with absolute confidence, which make the horse not only suffer and tolerate any rider, but also obey his or her orders.

Application of these methods should be perfect. These are the shameful "secrets of mastery" in ES. There is no room for controversy with all of the physiological, anatomical and scientific data, and excellent photo materials that illustrate them. Certainly, I did not want to create an impression that neurocranialis shock free application of bits is not fatal to the horse. Any bit usage leads to destructive processes in the organism and results in severe pathologies. But this article explores bit methods for inflicting neurocranialis shock which is the foundation of basic techniques in ES.

There are more secrets to ES. Very rich and illustrative research material is provided on them too.

1. Beating up a horse.

2. Sitting position of rider.

Both (beating and rider sitting position) will be the focus of subsequent articles.

This material is not targeted at covering riders in the photos with shame. All of them ride according to ES Statute, FEI and FESR (federation of ES in Russia) requirements, not one of them was excluded from any competition for the application of neurocranialis shock. This article is an effort to investigate basic methods of ES, and isn't addressed to any one person, but to the ES system as a whole.

HACKAMORE

Let's take a look at the secret of the effect of the hackamore, sidepull, bosal, medikana, caveson, kapcung and Parelli or other brand of rope halter.

The main pressure of all these "tools" is applied to the almost "naked" os.nasale (nose bone), or to be more precise — on processus nasalis, the forwardly extended nasal appendix of the nose bone.

The area where the pressure of the working part of the rope halter, bosal, or hackamore, is applied is the joint of the nose bone where the two halves of the nose bone connect and become a flat joint.

A flat joint is the most vulnerable and fragile joint of all bone joints in the horse.

The flat joint that brings together the two halves of processus nasalis is astonishingly fragile and breaks under any pressure. It breaks with such cunning that it is not visible on a single x-ray, which is not surprising because there is no break in the bone itself. Instead, only the connecting tissues of cartilage are ripped, those that "glue" the flat joint. This type of injury is almost a fracture, although we need to make a distinction that it cannot be represented as a "fracture" in a definite sense, yet the symptoms are identical in most cases.

Those who want to make sure for themselves can do so on a fresh horse skull by breaking the flat joint that connects the two halves of the processus nasalis; it breaks from finger pressure.

As soon as the flat joint gets destroyed (it's a matter of a minute) under the pressure of hackamore, sidepull or rope halter, the separated processus nasalis bones begin to "wander around". The integrity of processus nasalis is demolished, the halves, as people say, begin to "play" from any type of pressure.

First of all, what echoes on the shift is n.infraorbitalis, a nerve that has a very thick branch going underneath the nose bone. The separated bone produces a mechanical painful and irritating pressure on the nerve and a branch of

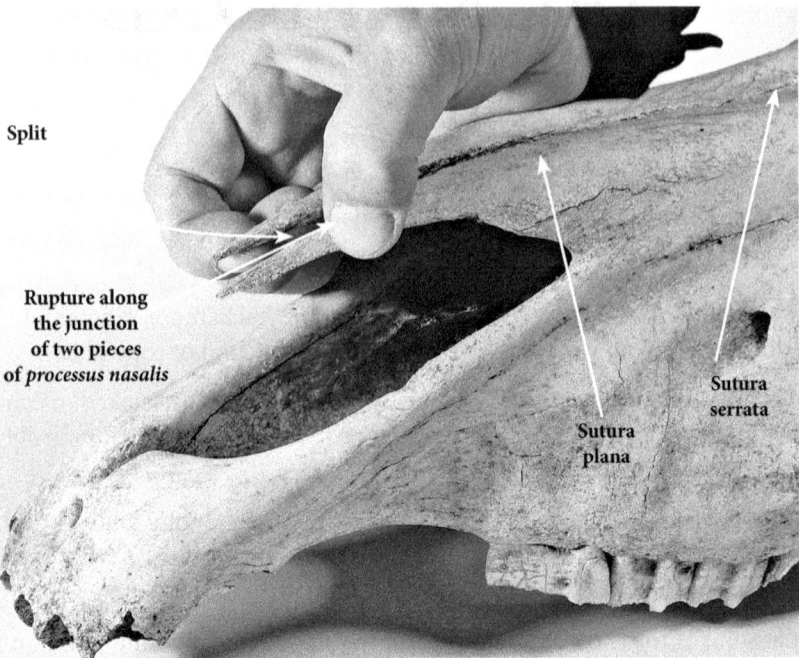

Split

Rupture along
the junction
of two pieces
of *processus nasalis*

Sutura
plana

Sutura
serrata

Photo 15. © Georgi Gavrilenko

Photo 16. © Sophia Spartantseva

the nerve appendixes that covers the nose bone from underneath — it deforms and tears, so the pain impulses go straight to the horse's brain. These pain impulses are immensely powerful. This is the secret of the effect of hackamore, rope halter and similar nasal equipment. Even a simple noseband, when tied hard enough, gives the same effect of separating the flat joint of the nose bone.

You can picture for yourself how great a shift occurs between the halves of the processus nasalis on any skull, even old, where combining cartilage has been boiled out or fell apart due to age. Having imagined the network of extremely sensitive nerves that are almost "attached" to the nose bone underneath being exposed to deformation and tearing – it's not hard to get a clear feeling about what pain is being produced. Very similar effects are caused from pulling to one side or another when using a hackamore, bosal, sidepull or rope halter.

BEATINGS

Strictly speaking, equestrian sport (ES) stands on two principal methods, as on two pillars. Apart from these, there are many tricks and methods, but these two pillars are the foundation for everything. Any "trick" is interchangeable with any other, any of these inconsequential "methods" can be distorted or removed from use – nothing in essence will change.

However, the two principal methods of ES are eternal, they are fundamental and basic. If either of them is removed, equestrian sport will cease to exist. All of its standards will become unachievable

The first method is NCS (inflicting the pain of neurocranial shock to the horse by use of an iron instrument fixed in its mouth).

The second is the beating of the horse.

This method of equestrian sport, second only to NCS in its importance to achieving sport standards, and a very relative obedience of the horse, is called by many names.

They can only be called "names" with great reserve; rather, they are euphemisms, which are shamefacedly covering the essence of the method.

The true name of the method frightens reporters and children, and sounds too unpleasant.

In the special language of sportsmen, this method is called "negative reinforcement", "to drive", "to make a correction", "moving off the whip", "punishment", "teaching the horse a lesson", etc., etc.

But the truth of this method is simply, the beating of a horse.

Though the word "simple" is not fully appropriate here. This is not simply beating.

Those who beat "simply", without an idea, without drilling to achieve the special skill of a sport – stay forever patrolling in muddy riding schools or chasing flies in the rooms of others' stables.

Photo 17. © Georgi Gavrilenko

Effective beatings require skills, competence, calculation, and have many nuances and aspects of application. Here we have the same kind of story as with iron.

If a snaffle bit or a curb, tucked into a horses' mouth could make anyone become an Olympic champion, then everybody would become a champion. But only a few become "winners", people with special moral, educational and character features, those who learned accurately, and callously to inflict neurocranialis shock to a horse by a blow with an iron instrument fixed in the horse's mouth.

Those who have mastered this method correctly (by the standards of ES) use it. But as we know, 99.9 percent of sportsmen spend all of their lives mutilating the horse and its mouth, but remain unknowns even in equestrian sport, even in spite of having the main characteristic, which helps achieve success in ES, total insensitivity to the horses' feelings.

With horse beatings everything is the same. If beatings had the magical quality to bring medals, ribbons and prizes to those who employed them, then there would be no sportsman or student who wouldn't be covered with medals like a fish is covered with scales.

But that is the catch, beatings create sport-worthy results only when they become formed into some method, the mastery of which is the most important condition of success in equestrian sport.

Ninety-nine percent of sportsmen employ these beatings incorrectly, without talent and in vain, not observing the special technologies of beating, not obtaining the necessary beating skills and not mastering the abilities needed to perform the most painful beatings. (Those that are the least noticeable to spectators).

This is what I mean by explaining that beatings practiced by EVERYBODY lead ONLY A FEW to the competition arena.

I say "EVERYBODY" with complete confidence. One hundred percent of sportsmen practice horse beating. It should be noted, for example, the rules of show-jumping competitions even allow public beatings of horses, limiting only the number of blows.

Public beatings are openly practiced at flat races, in harness racing, in driving, etc.

In the sport of dressage, horse beatings are practiced during all the periods of training for competitions. The tactics and techniques for the beatings are

Photo 18. © Georgi Gavrilenko

Photo 19. © Georgi Gavrilenko

Photo 20. © Sophia Spartantseva

Photo 21. © Georgi Gavrilenko

taught without any shame in all printed manuals about classical dressage and equestrian sport.

The human practice of inflicting severe pain by the use of a whip in response to the horse's unwillingness to comply with this or that fancy of a human is the most mundane and universal practice.

Inefficiency or reluctance to beat the horse in ES is a limiting factor to one's success.

However, if a sportsman is unsuccessful, there is no need to suspect him of honesty or kindness towards the horse. In most cases he is just like everybody else, he simply couldn't master even these two most primitive methods of control, inflicting NCS and beating.

Of course, there are cases when human qualities are a serious obstacle to a sporting career, when a very vague, weak sensation of unwillingness to torment a horse brings some "unconscious corrections" to the actions of a sportsman, and then he quickly becomes a "loser" in his work, or remains an amateur until the end of his life.

Sometimes he doesn't understand why his sporting carrier wasn't successful. But people like this are rare. Of course they exist, but the majority would like to beat the horse and destroy its brain with pain – expertly and effectively.

I won't describe here all the disgusting types of beatings. It doesn't relate to the topic of this research.

Also I don't intend to deny the crazy belief about the "necessity of punishment".

The reason for this belief is only the inborn stupidity, the categorical incomprehension of a horse and total lack of the slightest amount of "horse sense".

Normal people, those who are feeling, knowing and understanding the horse, know it without my assistance, and the audience in "swollen-head helmets and top hats" are not able to understand it. They lack the organ, which people "know" it by.

It's useless to persuade them. We have to recall a wonderful quotation from Diogenes from Sinop.

When some ignorant, narrow-minded-know-it-all turned to Diogenes with a suggestion for him, Diogenes responded: "If it were possible to convince you of anything useful and correct, I would certainly, first and foremost, convince you to hang yourself ".

As I have already said – in the world of equestrian sport it's common practice to substitute many different innocent words for the word "beatings". It's done partly for self-pacification, and partly because a sportsman, as a rule, doesn't understand what he does. Single or repeated blows he judges to be some sort of educational tool, absolutely normal and necessary, even serving some "higher" purposes and almost being beneficial to the horse.

Moreover, beatings following the refusal of the horse to grant one or another whim of a rider are an obligatory part in the training of a young horse when preparing it for sport.

I repeat, here I won't comment on the stupidity of these beliefs, I am not going to dissect the different kinds of psychoses. Apart from the normally accepted, prescribed beatings, there are other types, which are formally forbidden at competitions, such as beatings of the horse's eyes, head, genitals etc.

However, such kinds of beatings are practiced during training. Together with such "punishing" beatings, there are everyday, conventional beatings with everything within reach.

But this research will focus on the effects of NORMAL, permissible beatings, which are an accepted method in all branches of ES.

There is a categorical, furious denial of the fact that these permissible and OBLIGATORY actions of sportsmen (the beatings of horses) are not just painful, but a traumatic influence on a horse, causing extremely significant consequences to the physiology of a horse.

Naturally it's just an empty denial, generated by the remains of shame and desire to keep alive even a shadow of a myth about some possible "relationships" between a sportsman and a horse.

What IN ACTUAL FACT are the results of those beatings for a horse, those beatings that are an obligatory part of its preparation for the achievement of ES standards? Of course, any response without proof is worthless, therefore below I show the conclusion of the first official forensic studies in the history of the relationships between a human and a horse, the goal of which is stated in the very title of the report[3].

---

[3] These studies didn't take into consideration those severe inner traumas, which happen due to biomechanical "distortion" of horse's natural movements, when the whip is used. A special study will be devoted to this.

Photo 22. © Georgi Gavrilenko

Photo 23. © Georgi Gavrilenko

Photo 24. © Georgi Gavrilenko

Here, I assume, it's understandable that the goal of this research is to use a strictly scientific method to identify the extent of trauma caused by simple blows by a standard sport whip on a horse. This study, of course, doesn't show the how the horse's mental state has been affected as a consequence of such influence. Such facts, based strictly on scientific experiments don't exist.

However, based on the knowledge of physiological responses of a horse to pain and traumatic factors, based on how these physiological responses change aspects of its behavior, its mood and character, knowing the total dependence of horses' mentality and psychology on its physiological sensations, we can surely talk about extreme mental and psychic traumas, which are the consequence of pain and trauma (see Appendix 4, page 166).

The natural response of a horse to a blow is very quick, very sharp, and sometimes hysterical. Try to lash a free horse, not tied with halter, bridle, etc. The response will be immediate and very harsh.

Even a slight touch with a dry rod, which is not flexible and consequently has a tiny contact area with the skin (approximately 3–6 mm) and an equally small force of impact, will cause an extremely quick response of anger and fury. [4]

Horse skin is very thin, especially in the places where blows fall most frequently. For example, in the area of the muscle m. vastus lateralis its thickness rarely exceeds 2 mm, and closer to the inner side of the thigh — 1 mm.

But whatever the skin's thickness is, we have to remember that skin (dermis and epidermis) is generously supplied with nerves, making it a supersensitive organ.

The absence of a natural response to the blow speaks of either a horse's total oppression, or of its fear that a natural response will cause a much bigger pain, for example in the already damaged lumbosacral region.

In any case, a horse's submission to the pain from a lash signifies only fear of a stronger pain [5].

---

[4] A standard sport whip gives a "contacting area" 400 times larger than a chippy twig (approximately 20 cm, and up to 30 cm when the blow is especially "competent" — thanks to its flexibility).

[5] When buying a horse, you can easily find out how beaten he is. Whatever you are told (saying they "do not beat" is the fashion nowadays), it is enough to pick up any long straw and "unintentionally" wave in front of the horse's head. Any horse who knows a whip in action will immediately react.

Photo 25. © Georgi Gavrilenko

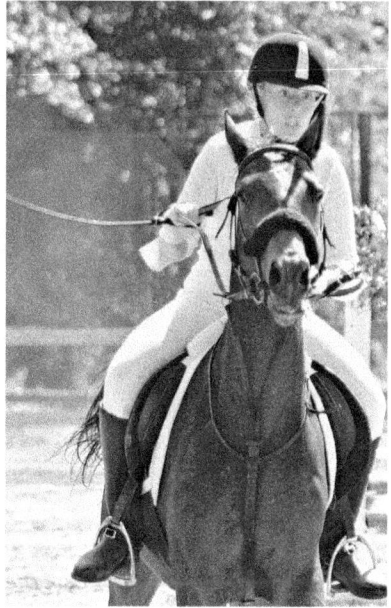

Photo 26. © Georgi Gavrilenko

Photo 27. © Sophia Spartantseva

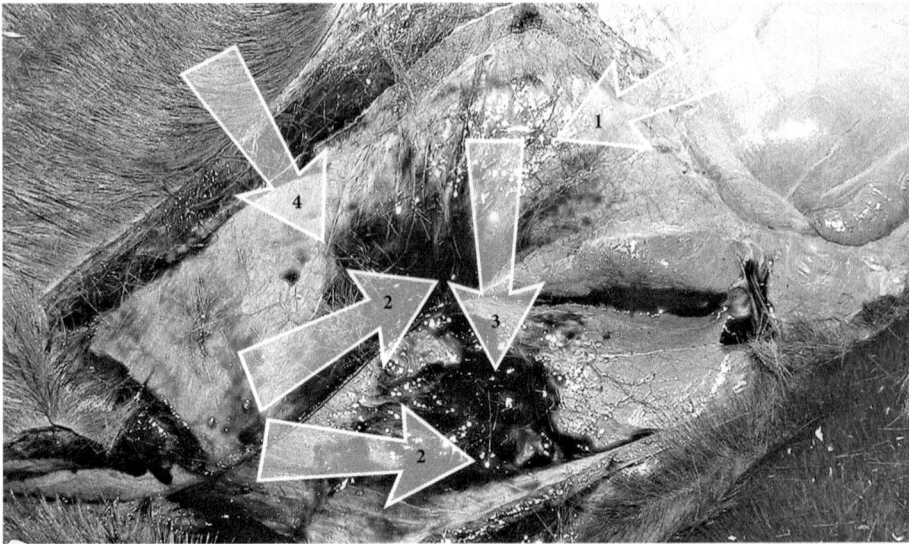

Dissection #255 (anatomic region — Hematoma hipodermaticum, H. intermusculare)
Group of heamatoma, typical hematoma caused by a whip blow of an average power
1. — Fascia superficialis; 2. — Hematoma hipodermaticum-1; 3. — Centrum hemat. (center of the hematoma, the point of the main blow; length: 7–9 cm above and 16 cm below); 4. — Vic. hemat. (periphery of the hematoma)

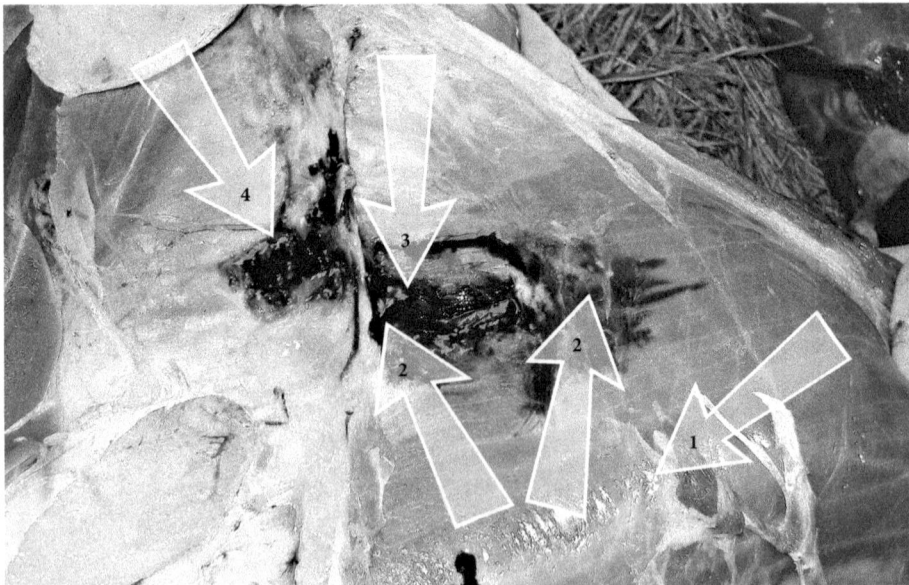

Dissection #256 (anatomic region – Hematoma hipodermaticum, H. intermusculare)
Group of heamatoma, typical hematoma caused by a whip blow of an average power

EXPERT MATERIALS DEFORMATION (BALLISTIC PLASTIC) UNDER INFLUENCE OF A TYPICAL WHIP BLOW USED IN SPORT

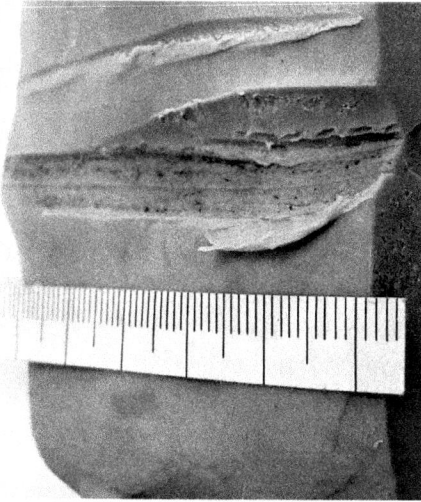

Depth and degree of deformation
A single blow

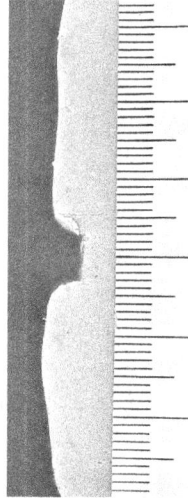

Depth and degree of deformation
A single blow

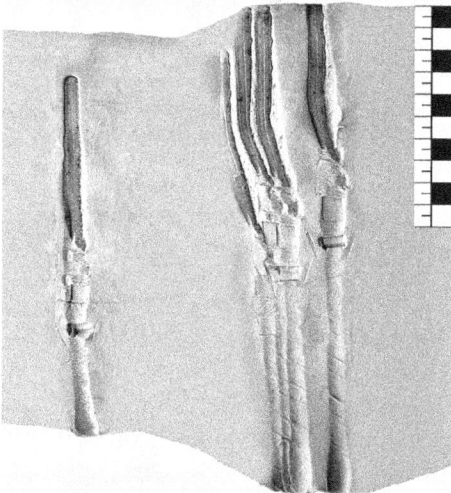

Depth and degree of deformation
A series of blows

Depth of deformation
A single blow

THE DENSITY OF BALLISTIC PLASTIC EQUALS THE DENSITY OF LIVING TISSUE

Clarifications for this segment.

Certainly, the force of the blow may be different, depending on the circumstances.

That's why different amplitudes were carefully calculated.

We know that children are taught to beat horses as well, practically from the first moment of their attendance at an equestrian school.

Naturally, the amplitude and the force of a child's blow will be somewhat different, but this was also taken into account. Typical blows were examined, not those which are practiced in "pathological" beatings, when a rider has a desire to "take it out" on a horse or really make it suffer from severe pain, but the so-called "educational" blows, "driving" blows, "moving off the whip", "teaching the horse a lesson", the ones which are officially permitted in the practice of ES.

Particularly because of that, the photographs in this research were ONLY taken during public performances and competitions.

Of course we also have pictures of training, "private" beatings, when all the spite of a sportsman against a "delinquent" horse was put into the blow, but the scientists only calculated and displayed the amplitudes of blows recorded at public performances and competitions.

It is no coincidence that I feel this document needs little explanation. The document itself will show the actual foundation of one of the main "secrets of mastery" in equestrian sport.

Everything seems clear. One more secret of mastery of equestrian sport has been disclosed. Certainly, any comments will be irrelevant after this scientific report.

What will be relevant is only to realize the extent of either stupidity, or innate and complete sickness of a person who has turned the traumatic beating of a horse into fun, into a "sport", or who has invented a sport, a fundamental part of which is the beating of a helpless, humble, paralyzed by pain in the mouth and cranium, horse.

While we're on the subject of investigating the relative extent of pain, sportsmen compare a blow to the horse to a half-hearted slap on their own legs. And to the absence of any particular feelings from this slap.

шечная), гл. гематомы
длиной -9-10 см.

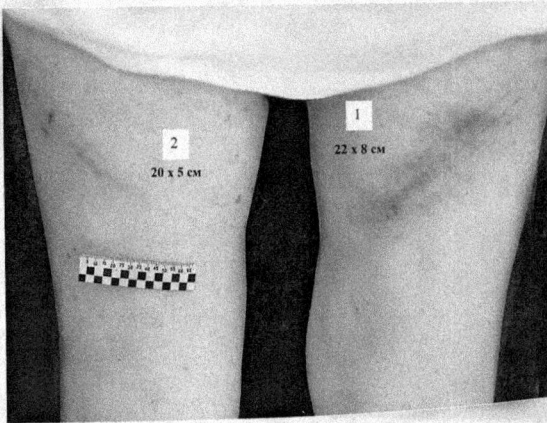

Место нанесения удара
хлыстом «спортивным», по-
верхностная гематома дли-
ной 22 см.A

Место нанесения удара
хлыстом «спортивным», вну-
тренняя глубокая гематома
(подкожная-межмышечная),
гл. гематомы -8-10 см.B

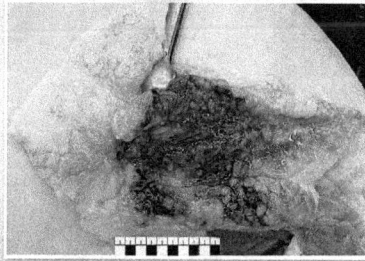

A — The point of striking with a "sport" whip, superficial hematoma 22 cm long.
B — The point of striking with a "sport" whip, inner deep hematoma (hypodermic-
muscular) 8–10 cm long.

Photo 28. © Sophia Spartantseva

Photo 29. © Sophia Spartantseva

Definitely this argument has a slight circumstantial value therefore we must address it.

To investigate this question we researched all cases of manslaughter or maiming by a whip known to Russian criminal science.

It's surprising, but such cases are plentiful. We choose the most indicative, with the best illustrational record.

In particular, in one of the archives there is an autopsy report of Ms.M__, murdered by an item, identified by criminal investigation as a "horse whip" (see page 43).

The sufferer was "beaten" to death with repeated blows by a show-jumping whip. Based on this autopsy report, we can tell with absolute certainty, that when real blows are given, identical to those which are given to horses in ES, severe traumas with significant amounts of damage are caused.

Unfortunately, the monstrous character of such photographs doesn't allow us to put the most horrendous (and the most important from the scientific point of view) parts in this book, but we certainly have them.

Pictures on page 44 give the full impression about both outer traces of the REAL effect of the jumping whip to the human body and the inner consequences of such lashes.

FALLING SICKNESS OF EQUESTRIAN SPORT

A HEALTHY WAY TO DIE

The whole principle of the "sport-riding seat" has already sent thousands and thousands of people to graves and wheelchairs, and it is clear that this trend will continue. Every year, every month and every day horseback riders will fall down; breaking hands, legs, ribs, spines, getting hit on the head with hooves, becoming disfigured, invalids and corpses.

There are too many examples of these falls, deaths and mutilations to not notice that they are very systematic and inevitable.

The mum, who takes her child to the horse riding club must know, that sooner or later she'll pick him up in an ambulance, and the drunk trainer will lyrically wave with his hand, saying "goodbye" to the latest victim of his idiocy and ignorance (see photo 30) because each trainer has his own "private cemetery".

This is a fact.

What is the main principle of the sport-riding seat, if we overlook the sportsmen's favorite idiotic phrases about "staying in balance" and "partnership"?

If we look at it honestly and succinctly, this formula is very easy to understand.

The sport-riding seat teaches a person how to stay on a horse AGAINST the wish of the horse.

Above all, AGAINST the horse's wishes, otherwise all these pain-inducing devices, without which horse sport and riding would be impossible, would be useless. (I'm referring to iron instruments in the mouth, nasal instruments of control, meters of straps, martingales, spurs, side reins, etc.) These instruments are still sometimes called "technical riding instruments", although already with some shyness, because the principle of their effect is already clear to everybody. And it is clear that they have absolutely no role in the "technique of riding".

Their function is to stop the rebellion of the horse against the painful mass on her back, which brings pain and discomfort in her whole organism. The instruments stop the rebellion by inducing a painful shock of a different strength. Their function is to paralyze by pain, to humiliate, to compensate for the absolute absence of the talent of the human to have normal relationships with the horse, to make her into simply a nice, stupid animal, who is subordinated by sudden painful movements and a simple mortal fear... of the pain.

Relationships, as it has already been shown many times by many people, do not need these or any other "instruments". That is already a proven fact. Every horse is phenomenally clever, and if you have a modicum of a correct relationship, simple respect for her physiological feelings, a horse can be controlled without any iron, nasal instruments or side reins. And if you have the knowledge and skills of the master — a horse is not just controlled, but also shows the phenomenally beautiful and effective collection and talent to do all (both simple and difficult) elements of Haute École.

Riders, sportsmen, and amateurs imagine themselves magnificent and romantic, by sitting on horseback they get that feeling of the beauty and high-performance that nature did not give them. But those who understand the principle of how these "riding instruments" work, see in these riders as pitiful, terribly scared people, who roughly sit on the horse who has been paralyzed by pain, and then use the most base methods, tormenting and beating that wonderful, thinking, living creature, showing off and breaking through their fear. They panic while trying to keep their secret, holding on to it by tooth and nail, and shouting to the world which already knows the truth about equine sport.

Some time ago, when the truth about the whole "romanticism" of equine sport and about the real principle of riding instruments wasn't SO widely known, it was easier for them to lie to themselves and to other people. Now it is nearly impossible.

The legend about equine sport has been destroyed. The evidence about the nature, and the real role of "riding instruments" has already been collected and verified by science. It is already well known and proven, that for equine sport you do not need any mastery or knowledge, you just need to learn several prim-

Photo 30. © Georgi Gavrilenko

Photo 31. © Georgi Gavrilenko

Photo 32. © Georgi Gavrilenko

Photo 33. © Georgi Gavrilenko

itive techniques of inflicting painful actions on the horse and to use them at the right time.

There is nothing more that you need.

Although, no, you do need to be able to do one more thing, to hold on to a horse. In spite of the painful actions of a rider, a horse is still a very sincere creature, who can always fight, and when she is already in a panic because of the idiocy and cruelty — she can even panic with huge destructive power, by which she can easily get rid of the "jockey" [6], and sometimes – can easily kill him.

A well-known guarantee of the rider's safety, when the horse cannot rebel — is the presence in her organism of many different acute and chronic diseases of the legs, spinal cord, chronic cranial pains because of the use of iron and many other diseases in her body. Surely, most horses used in "equine sport", are sick to differing degrees.

Assurances of local horse yard vets about the "horse's health" are at the least ignorant, but most of them are absolutely false, because these vets are serving equine sport and are financially interested in its profitable future.

I think that this is clear and does not need any more commentary.

The sickness of the horse gives "the jockey" some chances to finish his "equine sport training" or other riding activities without any serious accidents. But even in that case, in the presence of strong disease in an acute or chronic state — the horse, because of her sincerity, can still rebel.

And the "jockey", who has climbed on her back, has to "hold on". In that case, all the skills of the equine-sport seat are used (see photos 33, 34, 42).

This seat, translating this term into layman's terms, teaches a person how to behave when somebody hurls him out of his house. He learns how to hold on to the doorjamb, how to catch on the walls, how to rest on the threshold. In short, how to do all the things that will make the process of the hurling of the caddish guest more difficult.

Beginning, intermediate and other jockeys usually console themselves with the idea that frequent falling and trauma is the result of the fact that they are

---

[6] From now on I will purposely use this term as the word "rider" is too flattering for the people of this kind.

not experienced, that they had too few training sessions. They also persuade themselves, that with the experience that they'll get in their lessons — safety will come, that they'll stop falling and being traumatized. That's not correct.

Let's take the creature, who has, by equine sports standards, lots of experience; the very good and strong skills of the "equine-sport seat". More than that, for the sake of honesty, let's take as an example a very successful competitor, the idol of thousands of girls. For these girls who think that filling the mouth of the sick horse with iron, dragging themselves and their horses "from one letter to another", means doing "dressage".

I especially took a dressage jockey as an example, because she can be called a member of the most calm, non-extreme type of equine sport, in which (compared to show jumping or cross-country) there are not any sudden movements or extreme situations, there is a strictly fenced field, and one of the main conditions of the competitions is the fact that there are no distractions. People are not even allowed to sneeze there.

ANKY VAN *GROHNSVEN*

(translator's note: In Russian, *GROH* is the word used to indicate the sound something makes as it falls)

That's exactly what the primadonna of "dressage" is called even in German and Dutch equine sport magazines, which change the surname of this jockey into many different variations, and, to tell the truth, with always very funny results. And they always insert into her surname something that means falling, shamefully and tragically flying out of the saddle.

Remember — I specifically started talking about this lady. Her undoubted authority in the world of "equine sport" makes her endless flights and falls filled with a special idea and charm and illustrates that "Grohnsven" can fall from the horse in such situations where it seems that it is absolutely impossible.

She "gets a full mouth of the ground" (an old manege term) there, where it is absolutely not necessary or even possible. It is clear, that this lady is very authoritative because of her "standing" in equine sport. And because her falls can also be called very special. Let's have a look.

Just recently madam Anky made people laugh when she fell down from Nelson at a very prestigious dressage seminar, Paard en Passie, in the manege Martini Plaza in the city of Groningen. After that, Grohnsven traveled to Sweden

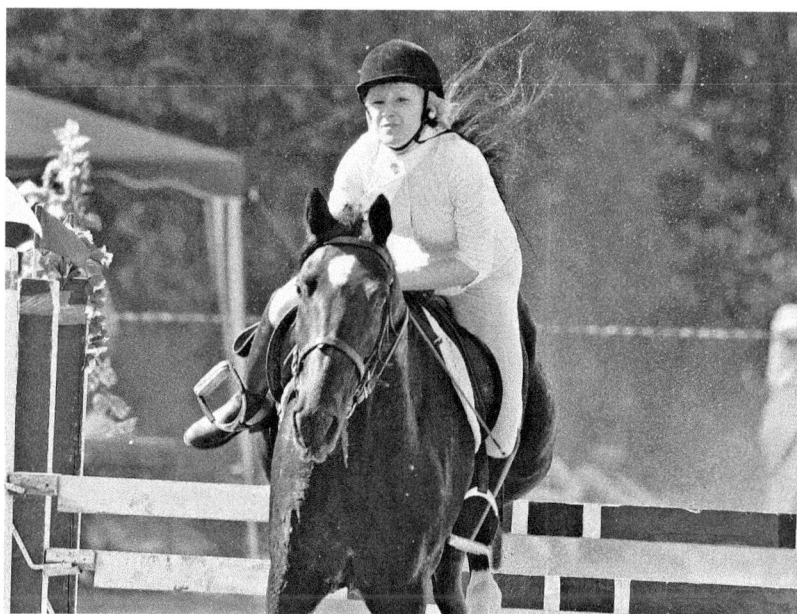
Photo 34. © Georgi Gavrilenko

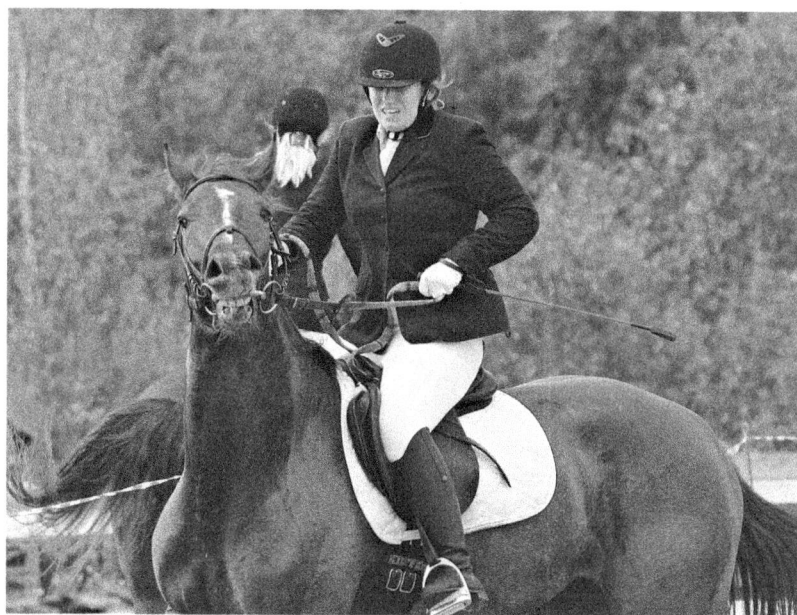
Photo 35. © Georgi Gavrilenko

to fall down in a very funny way in the Viking land from the horse Painted Black, riding before the eyes of the crowd in the same type of seminar.

Before that, the primadonna of dressage fell down in a competition from the horse Joker and broke her hip. And, of course, in the most "prestigious" competition — GROHNsven fell in the funniest way.

In the moment of receiving an award — her horse Salinero, crazy from pain and the typical dressage torture, — took control of the champion and just bolted out of the field. Anky shouted to the whole huge stadium, demanding help.

She fell down outside the manege, as the press maliciously reported — right on the trolley with ice cream and cola.

It is impossible to remember all her shameful and horrible falls, even if we remember only her falls during competitions, without thinking about all her falls during training sessions.

So, this champion demonstrates the typical disease of equine sport in all its beauty.

Although this lady uses all of the real and unimaginable pain-inducing instruments for stopping the rebellion of the horse and very professionally uses all the methods, that must, as she thinks, make riding safe and comfortable.

To tell the truth, it is very easy to notice that the more cruel and mean the "user" of the horse is, the more different instruments he uses. The quality and number of painful paralyzers offer more refinement.

It is funny, but equine sport nearly reached the level of zoophiles in the number of instruments used. These guys, for fulfilling their lust also designed many things, demonstrating, how the lust "to ride for fun" is similar to the lust of zoophiles.

Let's take the "Court gynecology" of V. Merzheevsky, St. Petersburg, Russia, year 1878, p. 264.

There we can see the description of such a case as: "18-year old village man V. Shubeev had sex with a mare; during that time the mare was locked in the stable and blocked with boards in such a way, that she couldn't move; her tail was tied up to the boards, under her body there was another board. Shubeev was standing on the boards without trousers and raped the mare." Surely, the poor mare was "wearing" everything that was possible, and all the boards, probably, had to be used because there were not any curb bits and side reins in the village.

СКОТОЛОЖЕЦЪ

There are notable transcripts of interrogations of the zoophile.

Zoophilia (also known as bestiality) is considered to be a grave crime in the Russian Empire.

Page 997: "Those who are discovered to indulge in the vice of bestiality should undergo the seizure of property and be banished to the remote parts of Siberia".

So, Schubeev was interrogated thoroughly. "Members of the court found that the interrogation subject looked feeble-minded, his eyes were dull and shifty. His head was wedge-shaped: the back of the head was well-developed whereas towards the face it converged. It was found out that his generative organ was well-developed while his whole body was immature for his age" (*page 265*).

"The governorate board took into consideration the answers Schubeev gave for the questions asked and decided that Schubeev with his deformed skull and other features should be considered half-cretin. Generally this man fitted the category of mental condition which is known as doltishness (stultitia)" (*page 267*).

It is clear, that, as we look at the collection of instruments, we can say that the village man Shubeev and the Olympic champion are drastically afraid of the horse. And this fear very artificially induces the strong adrenaline-induced wish to have "contact" with the horse.

A bit later, during the inquests of the village man Shubeev, which are also written about in the work of Merzheevsky — this fear is already clear and evidential.

This fear — this horrible panic — we can see even in the printed articles of famous sportsmen. V. Ugrjumov (master of equine sport, the champion with an important title in horse sports yet one that is meaningless in the face of the truth) honestly says, that he often "could not stand on his feet before riding due to stress" (simple fear). Such reports fill nearly all articles about equine sport. In most photos we can see not just fear on the sportsmen's faces, but clear panic (see photo 30, 35, 36).

In sportsmen's articles — it is also panic, tears, panic again. Shouts about adrenaline. Descriptions of how they're taught to "show the animal who's boss", and nerves again, falls, falls, falls, panic again, but again and again we can hear talk about the adrenaline.

It seems, that you're dealing with adrenaline drugs, when the lust to "ride for fun" always needs an atomic dose of pure fear. It is clear, that among cross country jockeys 1/3 of competitors involuntarily urinate during competitions. Other jockeys usually do this before they start.

In the secret articles of the circus master, we find that young circus workers are taught that "working with horses is much more dangerous than with tigers".

There are hundreds of methodical books about the psychological preparation of sportsmen, where we can see the description of shaking legs, the feeling of the "disobedience" in the near future, special pre-ride jitters, many terms.

Fear of the horse, of her rebellion and fury, nobody can keep it secret. She is a mystery to the sportsman, which makes him afraid. Fear, and nothing else, forms the base of the equine-sport seat.

This fear is also seen on the face, and in the movements of sportsmen. This is also the main reason for the fact that equine sport and falling from the horse always go together. But there is one more reason, no less serious than fear.

The reason is that all equine sport "training sessions" teach a lot more about how to fall, than how to hold on to the saddle. Any session of "equine-sport riding" gives the jockey negative experiences.

Believe me, it doesn't happen because the author of this article wants it to happen, it's just because of the strict laws which govern reflexes that were discovered and evidenced by the scientist I. P. Pavlov.

It's impossible to debate this.

Soon, falls due to "lack of experience", that seem to be natural — change themselves to the falls the main cause of which is training and experience.

It sounds unbelievable at first, but it is an absolutely natural thing, because, in practicing mistakes, it is easy to make them automatic and they'll become your "style", which will always end with falls, traumas, and death.

More than that, these mistakes are inevitable, because any type of equine sport makes a horse panic, ready for any provocation to make her not-surprisingly angry.

MALICE OF THE HORSE

It is usual to not think and not talk about this very simple and natural factor, about this elementary psychological reaction of any mammal to pain and discomfort. Both equine scientists and vets say nothing.

It must be remembered, that NOWHERE and at no time has any methodical book for "jockeys" talked about the elementary MALICE that a horse feels because of the rider's actions.

There is nothing to prove there. The inevitable aggressive actions, which affect the horse's physiology and nervous system, are too visible; the natural psychophysiological reaction of any mammal to such actions is known too well.

It is clear, that a horse for the sportsman is a stupid cow, which can be programmed with a dose of pain, but even the stupidest cow can become angry.

But even this fact is usually not discussed.

Stereotypes that dictate that the horse is a programmed piece of meat without thought or feeling do not let them think about such a simple thing as natural malice. The sportsman thinks that he can just use pain to program this very stupid piece of meat to make it fun.

Sportsmen even imagined many idiotic fairy-tales about how this meat likes to be tortured, and after that to be decorated with colorful pieces of ribbon.

Photo 36. © Georgi Gavrilenko

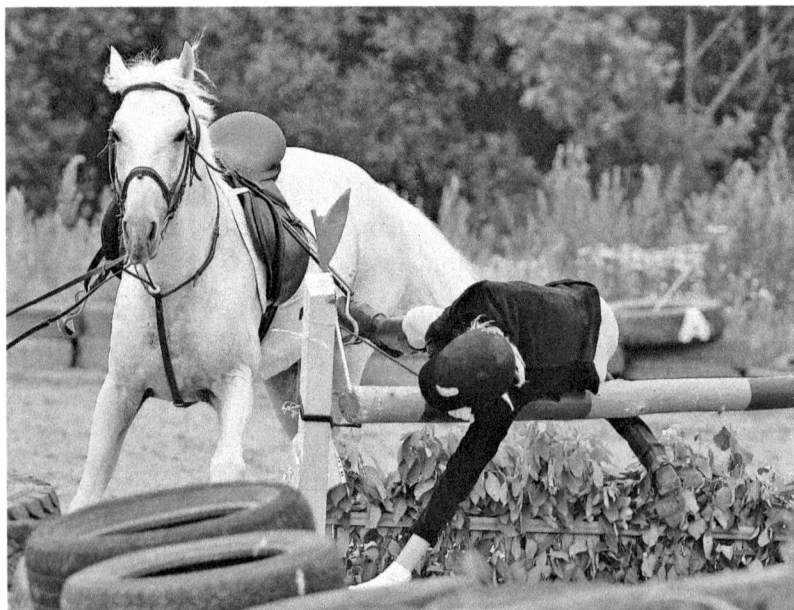

Photo 37. © Georgi Gavrilenko

And they even feed each other these fairy-tales in horse yards and on the pages of popular equine periodicals[7]. And that's the wrong thing to do.

The horse, because of her phenomenal intellect and sensuality always imagines many different ways of getting rid of the "jockey". And, because of panic, using her wonderful intellect she's creating the situations that beginners always recognize as bad cases.

Think about it, what is taught during the training sessions of dressage elements and jumping over painted sticks? What does the horse learn how to do?

They teach the angry horse (who feels pain and discomfort) to resist and rebel, to "catch" any weak moment in the human's behavior, and get rid of him with some extreme movements, and the "jockey" is taught to be scared of the horse and her movements.

This fear, this absolutely normal display of the self-preservation instinct — makes the human exhibit a very powerful reflex, which becomes permanent.

His body learns to be afraid in spite of all the magic words and psychological preparations. The "jockey" learns to clutch on the horse, to shake, he nearly gets convulsed.

I'll repeat again — the human, who is afraid of the horse, who is always afraid to experience the horse's rebellion, revenge, and extreme movements — learns to be afraid with the whole body. He learns to make his body "wooden". So, he is always learning how to fall.

I hope that it is clear why these two terms — "wooden body" and "fall" are very close.

So, during each training session (with a trainer of any qualification) — many negative qualities are learned and set, and also the skills of being afraid of the horse and her sudden movements.

And, as a result — endless falls.

If the human accepts the horse as a huge living piece of meat, whose emotions he does not understand, the same as her feelings and thinking, if the horse is

---

[7] Note that sportsmen believe the complex story created to make it seem like the horse is having a positive reaction rather than believing the simpler explanation that the horse is having a negative reaction to the rider's actions.

accepted by a rider as something that must be "restricted", and who is possible to deal with only with a painful instrument in her mouth or with stupid reflexive training, there will be no relationship between the rider and the horse, in spite of all the nice words about "contact".

The feeling of "danger" of the horse and horseback riding always can be seen in the funny riding helmets, body protectors, and the talk about Safety Procedures.

Also, the unhealthy atmosphere of an HRC (hire riding club, a place where horses are rented to ride) plays its role, where sportsmen walk into the horse yard with their faces pushed back from being hit with the hoof or the back of the horse's head sporting new traumas every day. All this only solidifies the fear of the horse, which always shows itself in the sport's seat. And finishes with the next fall or trauma. And this will always be a part of equine sport, as long as it is still alive.

There is one more illusion, the illusion that experience and time spent with horses, factors which form the "experienced horseman", also prevent some traumas and accidents. But this is also false.

Nowadays, unfortunately there are no specialized traumatological statistics, but now also there are very few people who can be called "professionals" even in that horrible, "equine sport" meaning of this word.

Although, the absence of modern examples is not the end of the world. There are many old recorded documents about those facts, about which traumas people got who were professionally working with horses: cavalrymen, coachmen, horse-riding firemen etc.

These documents are, probably, the correct thing to read. Let's take, for example, the academic works of the "Surgery herald" of professor N. Velyaminov in the year 1887. Let's take just one book out of 18 understanding that these written facts are just a half of a percent of the real extent of traumas of such types (see page 63).

P. 77: "A soldier of the 37th art. Brigade Nikifor Zjuzin on 5th of July 1881 (during the camp set up in the village of Krasnoe) got the hit on the right side of the head with the hoof of the horse that he was saddling." In spite of the fact that at 10 o'clock in the morning, under full anesthesia, the repair of the broken part of the skull was made, several hours later Zjuzin died. This case is described by the head doctor of Life Guard's Horse-Grenadier's regiment."

Photo 38. © Georgi Gavrilenko

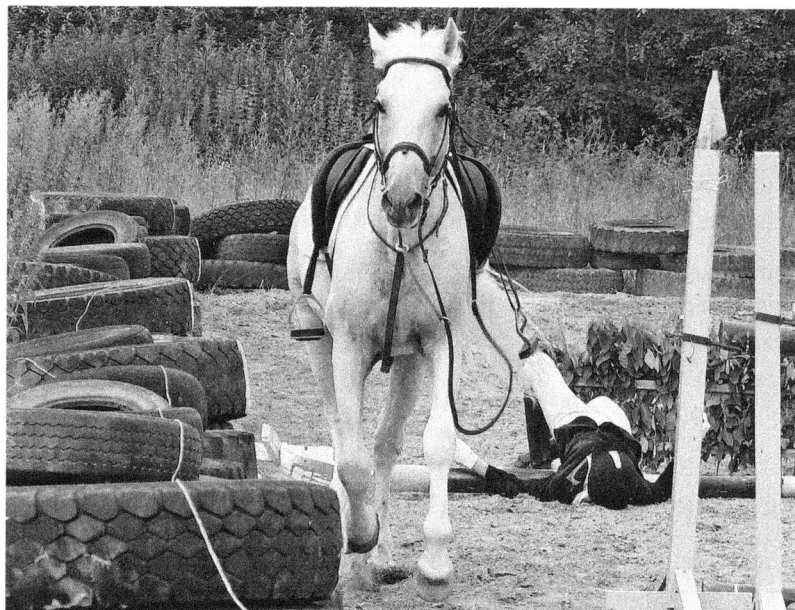

Photo 39. © Georgi Gavrilenko

P. 81: "At 8:30 o'clock to the Krasnoselsky hospital, the gunner Lb. Gv. Horse-Artill. Brigade Ivan Smordov was brought having been hit with a horse's hoof on the head at the waterhole. During the investigation the following things were found: in the area of the left temple there is a torn wound and pressed broken bone, and the top part of the ear is torn out."

On the top illustration on the following page, you can see the real size of the destroyed part of the temple bone.

P. 392: "I. Arhipov, kr. 23 l. light coachman. Was hit in the head with the horse's hoof, was brought to the hospital in shock."

P. 396: "D. Dmitriev, kr. 12 l. Was hit in the area of the left eye with the horse's hoof. In shock. The top part of the eye region is separated from a cracked bone and pushed inside.

P. 405: "G. Stepanov, kr. 65 l. light coachman. Hit with horse's hoof. In the right crown area there is a hit-torn wound, in the bottom of the wound small pieces of bone can be palpated. After opening the wound, the broken crown bone was found, with the pieces of bone pushed inside the skull. Died 48 hours after being brought to the hospital."

P. 419: "N. Cherevko, working coachman of the Kiev fire brigade. Was hit in the head by the fire brigade horse. On the protrusion of the right crown bone, four cracks are seen with the bones pushed inside."

Believe me, this sheet may be endless, but I think that there are already enough facts to be sure that "professionalism" does not save a person from anything and that the skills of traditional horse torture do not guarantee any safety.

To tell the truth, in that time the horse's hoof was called a weapon and was always remembered as one of the main traumatic factors of that "equine era". For example, on *p. 621* it is clearly written: "In case of limited breaks of the skull, which are made with the axe, sable or horse's hoof – trepanation is especially recommended."

TALK WITHOUT AN IDEA, OR THE HOMONYM GAME

It is clear, that the destruction of equine sports of all types is the simple, undoubted duty of the human for the horse. But doing this duty absolutely does not mean that it tries to enlighten sportsmen, those who "love to ride for fun" or "half-breds" (by half-breds, I'm referring to those philosophical riders who

ночь провелъ почти безъ сна. П. 56, малый, слабый. Безсознательное состояніе; по временамъ стонетъ и охаетъ. Въ 10½ час. утра, въ наркозѣ мною
произведена трепанація; долотомъ и элеваторомъ удалена вся вдавленная
часть кости, ради чего рана расширена кпереди и кверху. (См. рисунокъ,
изображающій въ натуральную величину удаленную часть кости). Dura ma-

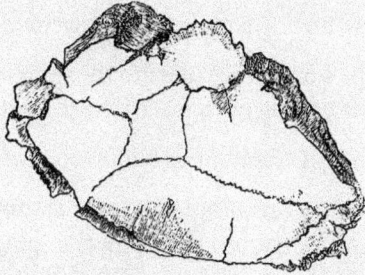

ter дѣла, темнокраснаго цвѣта, морщиниста и вдавлена; это послѣднее яв-
леніе, впрочемъ, скоро исчезло, она стала тверже и выпятилась въ отвер-
стіе черепа. Кровь и сгустки между dura и костью удалены, вся полость
раны облита 8% растворомъ хлористаго цинка, рана тампонирована іодо-
формной марли, наложены стягивающіе швы и давящая антисептическая по-
вязка на всю голову. Послѣ операціи пульсъ 80; безсознательное состояніе
продолжается.

кускомъ правой верхней челюсти; линія перелома идетъ чрезъ правое antrum
Highmori; кромѣ того, лѣвая верхняя челюсть переломана вдоль—линія перелома
идетъ между первымъ и вторымъ коренными зубами до глазницы и проникаетъ
чрезъ proces. palatinus и os palatin. sin.; нижнія стѣнки глазницъ разрушены;
proc. nasales maxil. sup. и носовыя кости совершенно раздроблены; оба proc.
pterygoidei и носовая перегородка тоже раздроблены; такимъ образомъ, верхняя
челюсть представляетъ 3 большихъ куска и много маленькихъ; далѣе нижняя
челюсть сломана въ двухъ мѣстахъ: одинъ переломъ между лѣвымъ клыкомъ и
рѣзцомъ и, кромѣ того, отломъ proc. condyloidei, причемъ линія перелома идетъ
изъ средины incisurae semilunaris къ angulus mandibulae. Переломъ основанія черепа: линія перелома начинается на правой сторонѣ у передне-верхняго края
большаго крыла, идетъ черезъ верхній уголъ alae magnae, по шву squamae съ
большимъ крыломъ, опять черезъ большое крыло, foramen rotundum, между proc.
clinoideus medius и antic. dextr., по sulcus opticus, foramen opticum sin., fissura
orbitalis sup. sin., черезъ мѣсто соединенія alae magnae съ лобною костью, опять
черезъ верхній уголъ лѣваго большаго крыла и оканчивается въ швѣ чешуи съ
большимъ крыломъ [1] (a). Другая трещина, продольная, идетъ изъ sulcus opticus
(отъ линіи поперечнаго перелома) черезъ tuberculum ephippii, sella turcica, къ

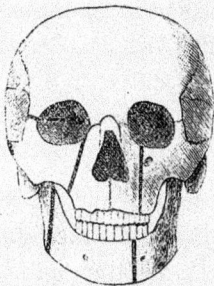

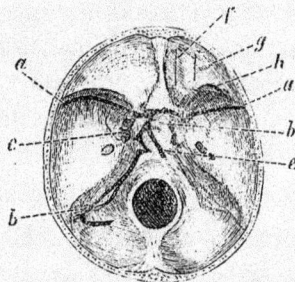

мѣсту прикрѣпленія верхушки пирамиды и оканчивается въ foramen lacerum
ant.: верхушка пирамиды надломлена, далѣе пирамида отдѣлена отъ затылочной

Photo 40

seem to understand something but cannot stop "taking their riding drugs".)

Doing this duty, fortunately, does not mean any necessity or even chance to talk to the sportsmen or any other people that were mentioned before.

Here, in this war "for the horse" the rules are the same as in billiards: you must not beat on the ball that you want to put to the pocket.

You can and must beat only the neutral ball(s).

It means that it is possible to accomplish the strict, non-compromising, slow and massive destruction of equine sport, by changing the public's opinion, and in this way taking equine sport out of the realm of prestige.

An enlightened public opinion will kill equine sport.

It must be remembered, that any talk about horses by a sportsman, rider or "half-bred" — is just a homonym game. Homonyms, as it is well-known, are words that are written and pronounced in the same way, but they have absolutely different meanings.

Here is the easiest example.

"Ball" as a round object used in games in sports and "ball" as a formal social event. Or "plan" as something you intend to do and "plan" as a technical drawing.

Nearly the same game happens when you try to talk to the sportsman-rider or to the "half-bred" about the real nature of his actions against the horse, or about the details of management, or equine history, or even hoof care. The word "HORSE" becomes the homonym, in which WE and THEY have absolutely different ideas. There is nothing similar between these ideas, not one point of contact or even accidental similarity. Any talk becomes absolutely useless, because people talk, pronounce a word, and then fill it in with an absolutely different idea. Any talk turns into a waste of time, a homonym game, a theatre of the absurd.

Of course, there is some hope for the equine sport seat, which often lessens the numbers of those who accept the horse as a nice programmed piece of meat who must serve a human's activities, or have other opinions, which differ from the School's.

But, to tell the truth, I put much more hope on Einstein and his great formula for widening the human's intellect: "The intellect, that once has widened its borders, will never come back to the old limits."

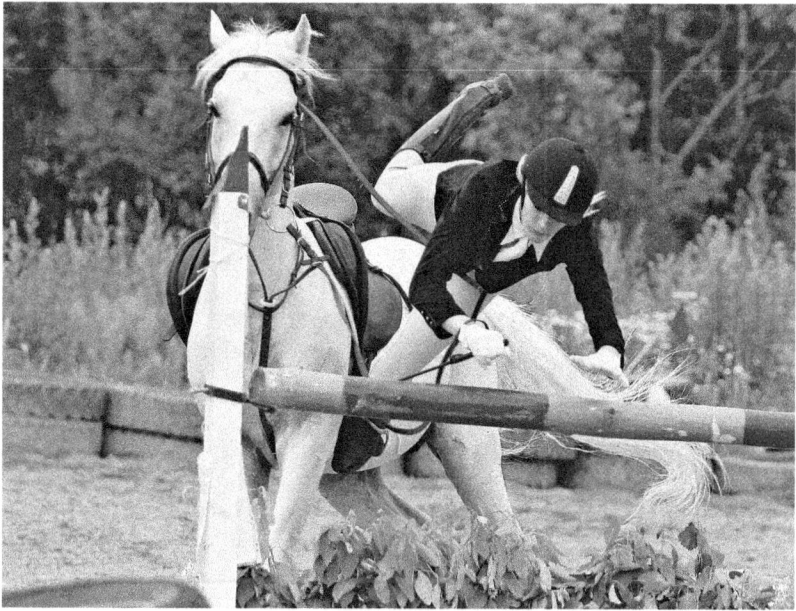

Photo 41. © Georgi Gavrilenko

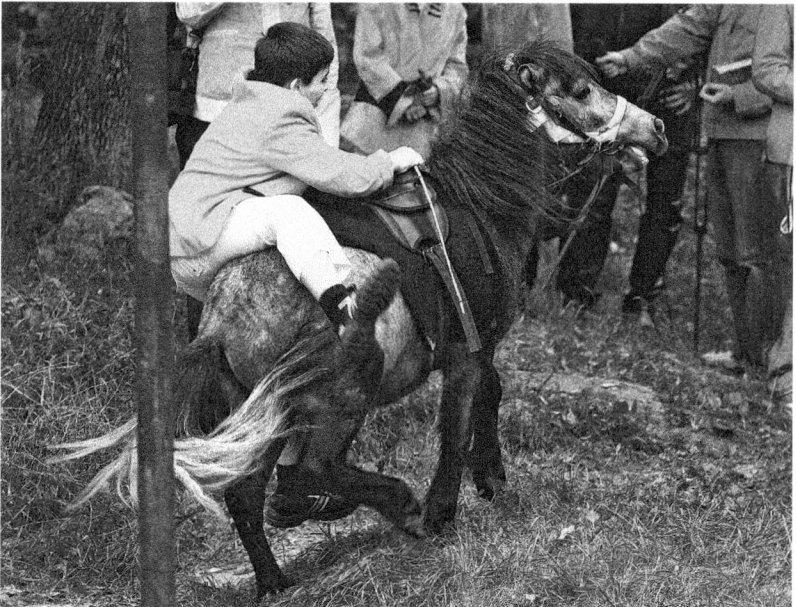

Photo 42. © Nevzorov Haute École

Photo 43. © Georgi Gavrilenko

Photo 44. © Georgi Gavrilenko

This law — is a truly fatal sentence to equine sport and other "jockeys".

And it has already started working.

P. S. Of course, they can be grabbed by the back of the neck with facts and science, you can rub their nose into it, as you would do with a puppy who peed on the floor. But they would shirk and wriggle. And they would stick to their opinion.

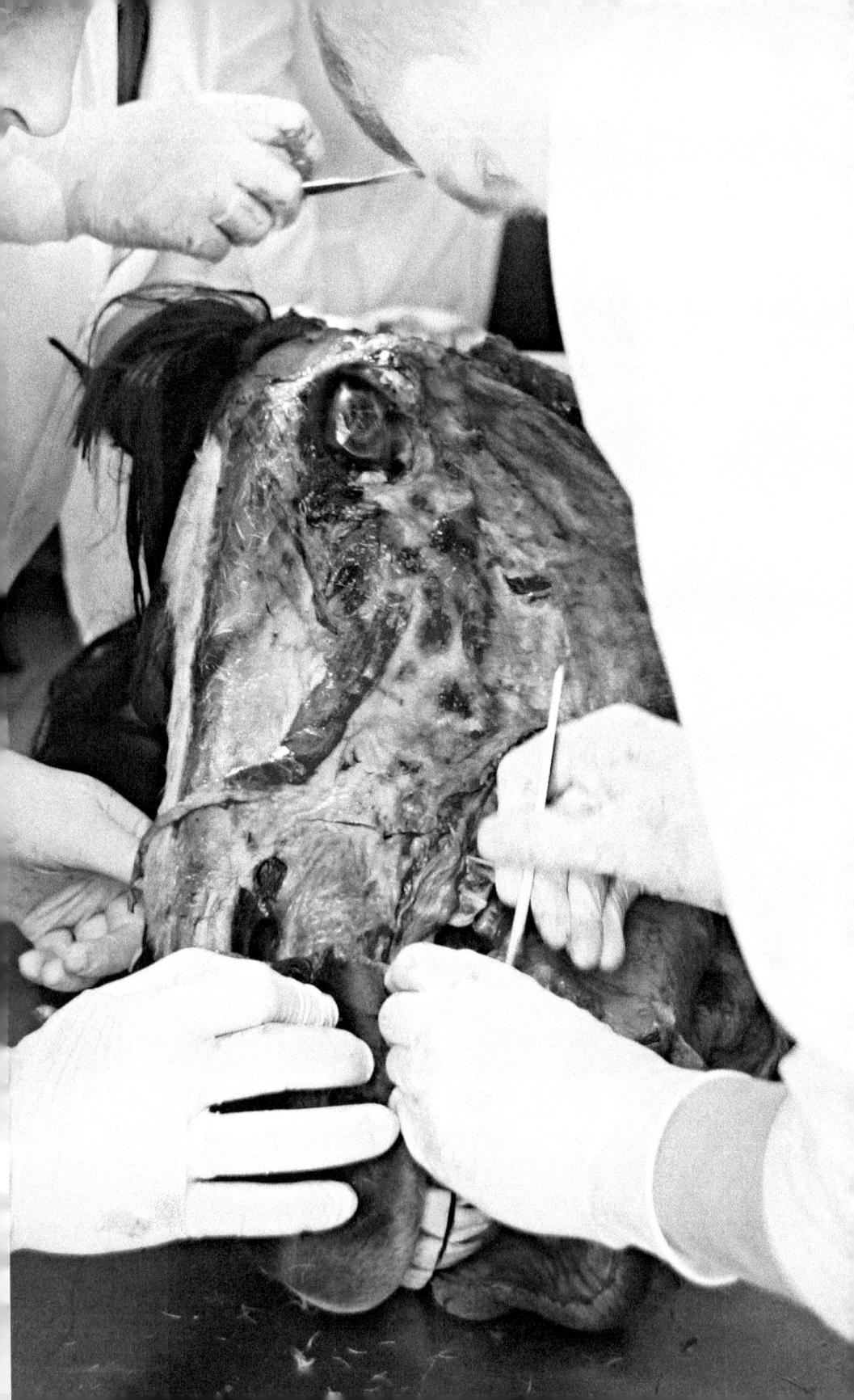

DRESSAGE: LET'S DOT THE I's AND CROSS THE T's

Among the usual merchandise of sex shops such as handcuffs, collars, big flexible phallic-shaped whips, spurs, strapped facemasks, black bodices and panties, there is a black BDSM (Bondage and Discipline, Sadism and Masochism) head mask.

Or rather it is not just a head mask, but a full hood mask which wraps completely around the head, face and neck. This mask may blindfold the wearer, in those varieties without eye slits (I ask you to remember this fact).

But this mask always has a perforated mouth. The perforation can look like "BARED TEETH" or a "SMILE".

In the article "Fear and Anger" those whose face is tightly encased within the BDSM head mask were considered. They are show jumpers and their masks sport the "BARED TEETH" perforations. Their faces are always awry belying an obvious fear of the horse and with a specific furious intensity of "sport". Now let's consider those, whose masks show the "SMILE" perforation. This is so-called dressage.

It is no accident that I referred to the product line of a sex shop. This is the most direct and clear analogy, full stop. As a matter of fact, when we talk about equestrian sport, it is our DUTY to realize what makes those people who practice it tick.

Let's look at the current calendar. It is 2007 now.

It is clear that for a sensible relationship with a horse there is no need for any accessories, straps, or metal tools in the horse's mouth or on a man's feet, or for the barbarically cruel effect of cords, clasps, and rings — in short, all the types of equipment of equestrian sport. The uselessness of all these things has been scientifically proven and is common knowledge.

All over the world, masters of horse education exhibit shining examples of communication with a horse without any painful tools. They refused on principle to use any devices that would cause pain in a horse's mouth, or to their nose, poll, sides, croup muscles and legs.

Currently there are enough masters (of different levels) of this orientation in the world, that we can talk of the fact that the system is generating, for example, performance of such elements as courbette, piaffe, and balancer by a "naked" horse. This is not an illustration of special gifts but just an ability to bring out the natural friendliness of the horse, his quick-wittedness and talent.

I have to say that my pupils overtake their teacher and soon will surpass. The story is the same with the other masters who refused to cause pain to a horse based on principle. There are many of them and their methods are effective as well.

It appears that all things are possible. The beauty of riding [8], training in hand, play, intricate exercises and High School elements are possible. Friendship, true friendship with the horse is possible. Everything is possible.

This is the path where bits and whips do not torture the horse; no one beats him or pricks and prods with spurs; no one tears apart his mouth, lungs and tendons. This is the path where the horse is not driven with fabulous speed to invalidism and death! This is the path of love, truth, honor, sense and great results.

In principle, when people who sort of "love horses" (according to their own estimation) see that they must pull off all barbaric mediaeval tools from their horses, the tools which have only one function - to control a horse through causing severe, paralyzing pain, those "horse lovers" will be bound to make friends with the horse, to create the relationships which enable them to show this very "love" in full.

But an absolute phantasmagoria occurs — an illogical and wild one.

"Horse lovers" such as show jumpers, dressage riders, eventing riders, owners of horses for hire, and amateurs (otherwise known as "PO", or "private owners", those who ram down on sore horse backs with their bottoms, never knowing for what reason), foam at the mouth whenever this path is mentioned.

---

[8] Now I fully rejected horseback riding. The horse is not intended for riding even in the slightest degree. Not physiologically, not anatomically, not psychologically. And this realization is based first of all on the results of long term research.

Photo 45. © Sophia Spartantseva

As it turns out, without the bit and all sorts of straps which serve to torture the horse, when they have no way to inflict pain and injury on the horse by forcing him to go in for so-called sport or its amateur shadow, when they have no cause to dress in special clothes like red hunt coats and hunt caps, they lose interest in a horse at once. The horse becomes pointless for them.

It's hard to believe but it's true!

About 85 percent of the polled sportsmen candidly acknowledge that if equestrian sport was forbidden or eliminated in some other way, horses would become absolutely uninteresting for them.

Moreover, they debate in all seriousness the horse's right to exist in the case of prohibition of equestrian sport.

Is it absurd? Sort of…although psychology (specifically sexology) researched this phenomenon long ago. Now I have to advert again to a very unpleasant analogy for some readers. (My profuse apologies).

The experiments were carried out in Salzburg with couples and groups practicing so-called BDSM.

In the course of experiment it was found out that the participant lost interest in a partner without a mask, collar with spikes, shackles, strapped bodice, or in a partner who banned any beating.

The "horse lovers" have approximately the same reaction when they are deprived of an opportunity to inflict pain on a horse and the use of their customary habits.

I realize the extreme crassness and directness of this analogy and I apologize to all who might be offended by it and its seeming impropriety.

But now everything becomes clear once and for all. Possibly I can help someone to make sense of the reasons which lead him (or her) to equestrian sport. If we answer the question: how did we come to this, we'll possibly be able to find the answer. We'll be able to understand why someone who has realized the nature of equestrian sport, engages in it, and why someone would stay.

There is another striking fact. Nearly 100 percent of the polled sportsmen and amateurs cannot explain intelligibly why they chose the equestrian sport rather than another sport. They try to get away with banal pretexts such as "it's beautiful" or "I love horses so much".

(Apropos, when you hear that the sportsman says "I do love horses so much", - you would do well to remember that Chicatilo "loved women so much". (*Chicatilo — a Russian maniac sort of like Jack the Ripper (translator's note)*)

But I do understand the senselessness of condemning all these people. I'm only trying to find out what incites them to get involved in equestrian sport. One may say, considering practitioners of BDSM and their psychological doubles from equestrian sport, it is very likely they all have deep inward causes for demonstration of this specific behavioral model.

Flogging kits, spurs, and laced up bodices are the breath of life to those people who buy them in sex shops. They cannot feel any strong sensations without all these props. Simple relationships give them nothing. Yes, the existence of other, normal relationships is well known for them, but they don't feel any interest in such relationships or are hostile towards them.

It is quite understandable. Normal, natural relationships are drab and boring for them… They need "exceptional" feelings — the hiss of a whip, anguished cries, pleading for mercy, the tears and blood of their partner, and above all — the feeling of pain they inflict on another person is a must for them.

But there is a strange statistical coincidence: there are as many people who believe that martingales, tiedowns or curbs are necessary to handle a horse… as those who are hooked on expressing love with the big flexible phallic-shaped whips, spurs… and the mask with "BARED TEETH" or a "SMILE" perforation.

Of course, this is just a humorous statistical coincidence and nothing more than that. But the similarities of psychological archetypes, motivations, degrees of aggression and almost all other characteristics are striking, let's face it!

There is even masochism (that is the desire to feel pain) as every sportsman knows about the inevitability of falls, injuries, fractures, dislocations, injuries to the face by the horse's poll and hooves, and other displays of aggression from the horse, who was driven into a frenzy by pain.

But the "sportsman" gets on the poor horse again and again. What for? He does it in order to experience a mortal "fear of the horse", "fear of injury" (the pain of highly probable trauma) again. He gets on the horse in order to drive her to hysterics with beating and pain in her mouth, to inflict pain and to experience "fear of the horse" and pain to himself.

We are starting the difficult analysis phase from this point. Everything seems to be right but something is still not quite settled. BDSM with its blood, whips, masks and chains is a voluntary thing.

The BDSM is founded upon "mutual consent". But in equestrian sport nobody asks whether the horse "wants" to do sports or not. They do everything by means of brute force, cruelty, beatings, sedatives, tools and other devices.

So we have a psychological analogy of a horseman and the sadomasochist. It sounds terribly unpleasant, I'm shocked too.

But each sportsman considers himself normal and sees nothing pathological in his passion for dressage.

And what is more, he sees nothing pathological in the "process" of dressage.

They regard the tools of dressage (bit, whip, spurs) as something natural, something they cannot do without.

But, it is curious that…according to the poll of the BDSM participants, they see nothing extreme or pathological either in the peculiarity of their actions or in other paraphernalia associated with BDSM.

In their view the whips, spurs and masks are something natural, something that must-be for them, and without all these things the very "process" is impossible.

Well, we've got an unpleasant, although explanatory, analogy but it is only an analogy.

Now, let us look at those people who cannot clearly answer the question: why do you participate in equestrian sport? They actually look for some very SPECIAL feelings in it.

But they are unable to admit it. But in accordance with our "unpleasant" analogy these special feelings are directly related to the gaining of strong pleasure from the infliction of pain on another being.

Following the "analogy" further, a crucial issue arises, we must ask if equestrian sport can really give such an exciting and complete experience from the INFLICTION of pain.

Does the horse really suffer? This is a serious matter, which requires scientific proof. Let us examine. But let's complicate the task. We will not analyze show jumping for example. Everything is obvious and too superficial in this kind of equestrian sport.

Jerking the reins, whips, beating of the bit on the teeth, blood, the horse's wheeze, awful hits of horse's legs against the obstacles when horse "ploughs" into fences, falls and overturns, all these things are visible to the naked eye and too evident, as well as in racing, driving and three-day eventing.

Our task is too easy in the way of evidence from these kinds of equestrian sport to be absorbing.

We'd better investigate so-called "dressage" which is considered the most dignified and decorous discipline of equitation.

There are no falls or flips and not any extremes in this kind of sport as the dilettante practices it. The horse's agony is not really visible at first glance.

Only an expert who knows how, where, and what to look for, can see that everything happening in the dressage arena is torture for a horse.

Let's take a look, too.

I will remind you we need to find out the truth about pain, about its power, degree and effect.

The type of people who practice the pastime known as "equestrian sport" won't tell the truth. Perhaps they don't know, don't feel, or... don't see it is one.

As I have already told you, the masks from aforementioned kit can be BLIND. Instead of the truth, they will tell us something about "unity with horse", "love of horse", "happy athletes"...

Anatomic, physiological, postmortem, and biomechanical examinations of the consequences of both classical and sport dressage methods can be summarized and produced as scientifically proven facts.

The works of professors of veterinary medicine and deliverances of doctors of veterinary medicine were summarized. They are: R. Cook, Professor of Veterinary Medicine, Honored Surgeon (USA); H. Strasser, Doctor of Veterinary Medicine (Germany); S. Skinner, Doctor of Veterinary Medicine (USA); E. De Buckeler, Doctor of Veterinary Medicine (England); I. Colloredo-Mannfeld, Doctor of Veterinary Medicine (Austria); Professor Zelenevskij, Director of Anatomy Department of Veterinary Medicine Academy (St. Petersburg), and many others.

The Research department of Nevzorov Haute École, together with experts of the Forensic Medical Examination Office in St. Petersburg: Professor V.D. Isakov, Doctor of Medicine, Deputy Chief of Forensic medical examination office for the expert department; Professor B.E. Sysoev, Doctor, Medical examiner of higher category, Candidate of medical science, and the Ballistic Examination Bureau: S.M. Logatkin, Candidate of medical science, Colonel of Medical Service, Deputy Chief of body armor facilities testing laboratory, have conducted studies of the effect of the bit on the nerves of the horse's head.

All of the results obtained during examinations and experiments are verified and certified by numerous necropsies (postmortem studies and dissections of equines).

On the grounds of the expert findings in these studies, necropsies, and dissections, it may be safely said that the principle effects on a horse in so-called "equestrian sport" who has been subjected to the principle of constant shocking pain, and methodical torture, are irreversible pathological changes to the horse's vital organs. What comes next is invalidism and a slow premature death.

No living creature in the world is inflicted with such strong and prolonged painful torture as the horse in equestrian sport.

Dressage, with its generally accepted methods, rests only on use of painful tools and uses pain as the main and only motivation, like all the other disciplines of equestrian sport.

Naturally, so long as this method of action is accepted as constant and the interaction of "rider-horse" is impracticable without it, there are significant abnormal changes that occur in the horse organism.

These changes can be easily identified both by necropsies after death and by clinical diagnostic techniques while a horse is alive.

But we will consider the necropsy results as absolutely indisputable and unambiguous, which strike out various treatments, arguments and discussions entirely.

It is the dissection that opens all the "secrets" of equestrian sport.

That's why I'm saying: "Let us ask the carcasses of horses killed by dressage.

They have nothing to hide but have something to say."

The extent, severity and nature of internal injury of a horse according to necropsy or dissection findings make it possible to decipher the pain code of such a discipline as dressage.

Rummaging the cold muscles, bared nerves, enormous stratified hematomas and dissecting joints and membranes, the picture of "the most elegant sport" becomes clearer in all its terrible clarity on the table in the dissecting room.

The cold piece that was a horse just this morning, is phenomenally understand-able and absolutely honest.

So, what exactly happens on the dressage training (or "battle") field? In accordance with all requirements and qualifying standards of any type of dressage, the horse is forced into false collection (with a violently flexed poll and engaged hindquarters) by means of special devices, lever force and other forms of pain.

What happens in a horse organism as a result of false collection? The first consequence of false collection is the full or partial crushing of parotid salivary gland (glandula parotis). This is the gland that primarily takes upon itself "the blow of vertical flexion" because of its location. It suffers most of all turns into a disrupted mass, into a solid stratified hematoma

The depth of hematoma as seen in different horses varied from 3 to 13 (!) centimeters.

But each of these horses had glands turned into mush.

The photograph shows clearly the upper subcutaneous layers are practically unaffected. Their color is natural; they haven't got any impact marks or signs of external blows.

This affected area is deeper, somewhere at a depth of one centimeter.

The following photos confirm — yes, this is a deep inner lesion that has been formed by a traumatic cause.

I give you a comparative photo of the other horse's autopsy findings. This horse sustained a lifetime of severe subcutaneous injuries. (When he was in agony in a terminal state, he strongly knocked himself against the walls of the stall.)

Look at this — a severe but subcutaneous hematoma. The depth of hematoma is about 3 millimeters, to be more exact from 1 to 3.

But in our case everything is different.

It is obvious that the trauma has originated from within, not due to external causes such as external blows or wounds. It is the gland that is located in this place, which actually has a "grayish-yellowish-pink" color in its natural state. Dark and damaged "dressage" color can be seen perfectly well in the photo of dissection too.

Prolonged constant squeezing of the parotid gland (as in forced collection) accounted for this inner lesion. The gland is squeezed between the caudal part of the vertical ramus of the mandible and the atlas. The gland structure is much weaker than any muscular tissue structure. It is easily affected. Five minutes of collection is enough to damage some horses.

Poor density of the gland (in comparison with the density of muscular tissue) cannot protect the arteries. The following arteries and veins are pressed and injured with varying degrees due to collection: condylar artery (condylaris), external carotid artery (carotis externa), great auricular artery (auricularis magna), superficial temporal vein (temporalis superficialis), external maxillary vein (maxillaris externa) and some other arteries and veins.

This is how it looks during trainings and events (view photo 46).

And this is how it looks during autopsy (view photo 47).

There are large quantities of affected and irritated nerves during the pressing of the parotid gland in collection. And practically all of these nerves are "sensory".

There are the facial nerves (n. facialis), internal auricular nerves, caudal auricular nerves in the "lesion zone" caused by collection, and the basic branch of the caudal auricular nerves. Frontal and lacrimal nerves are subject to an extra amount of pressure.

The effect of the crushing of all these nerves causes painful shock which is severe and stupefying. You can see a typical hematoma of the parotid gland, caused by dressage, in the photos. The different color of the strata denotes that hematoma has many strata and is "cumulative".

That is to say that the horse with profound and very painful trauma to the parotid gland (and the sublingual gland as well) has been repeatedly forced into collection, and goes on building the new strata of hemorrhages caused by compressed veins and arteries. By the way, this is a typical finding.

Besides the unbearable pain that the horse experiences (the list of affected nerves), colic was guaranteed for him from the moment his mistress had taken a fancy to try dressage.

I will briefly explain what colic is.

The death of every sport horse by colic is only a matter of time.

The crushing of the parotid gland by forced collection guarantees it. This leads to abnormal changes in the whole digestive system.

The chemical composition of saliva changes as the parotid glands - the largest of the salivary glands — are crushed and necrotized as a result of forced collection; the bit in the mouth injures the sublingual gland (glandula sublingualis polystomatica). The mandibular gland (glandula mandibularis) which, relatively speaking, does not suffer as severely, emits a seromucous secretion and its excess upsets the balance of chemicals in the saliva composition. Saliva tests of sport horses reveal cardinal differences between the saliva of a sport horse and that of normal saliva!

The rest is a technical matter. Acute stresses from pain and the effect of the bit, which is unavoidable in the life of every sport horse, leads to ulcers. The chemical changes of the saliva composition and its quantity leads to gastritis, colitis and others.

Gastritis, colitis, and ulcers lead to colic, which causes death. The process is so simple that it is unworthy of special discussion. Unfortunately, the outcome is predetermined.

When "sportsmen" try to whitewash themselves or rehabilitate the sport, they shout the names of the long-lived horses, those who were used in equestrian sport during a specified time of their life. The list is traditional, there are only a few names. They shuffle their names in different orders: Kvadrat, Druzhok, Sophist, Budynok... Druzhok, Sophist, Budynok, Kvadrat...

Usually when I hear these names I ask them politely, "More!"

Another five names of horses, those who were in sport but somehow managed to reach the age of 20 (of a horse's natural biological 40-year life span), arise with an effort.

I ask for "More!"

Once they pulled up the names of 15 horses!

Well, let us suppose (my princely gesture) that there are 100 of them!

God forbid, but the list of those who survived in Auschwitz, is dozens or even hundreds of times longer!

The quantity of survivors of the biggest "death factory", primarily oriented towards the mass murder of people by Nazis, outnumbers by a hundred times the quantity of horses who reached age 20 in equestrian sport! But this is sentimental talk; we have once again digressed from the research issue. Let's return to our subject.

Photo 46. © Natalia Bykova

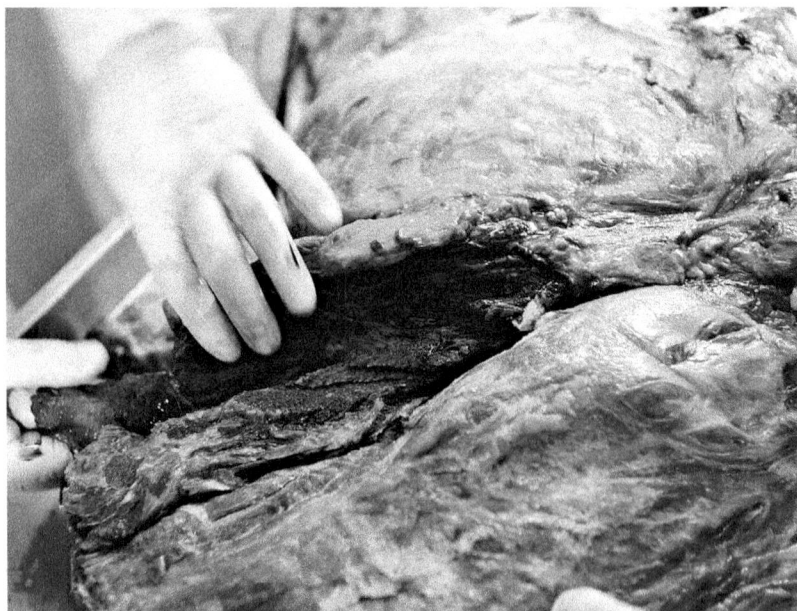
Photo 47. © Lydia Nevzorova

So, we've got the proven fact of the presence of intense and constant pain of the parotid gland of a dressage horse. There are no doubts due to the character of the lesions. During its development, any animal that breathed was openly and continuously tortured. But there is one more factor.

Due to forced collection, injury of the atlantooccipital membrane (membrane atlantooccipital dorsalis et ventralis) is unavoidable.

The membrane tissue is delicate and thin. Its tears and ruptures do not really cause distress to a horse. Minutes of forced holding of the head in a "vertically flexed" position is enough to tear or injure the membrane tissue.

But! As soon as the membranes are torn (and this is the inevitable sequel to collection) the defense mechanism that protects the spinal cord is lost.

The membranes shield the great foramens between the occipital bone and atlas during the flexion and extension of articulation.

The most unpleasant thing is that the destruction of atlantooccipital membranes, and the membranes over the atlas and axis junction, free the so-called dens axis (lig. dentis dorsalis et ventralis), which starts "attacking" the spinal cord from below.

The painful sensations in this area are extremely severe.

By the way, most respectable anatomists and pathologists, in regards to the amount of pain experienced by a horse, place membrane destruction ahead of the tragedy of the parotid gland.

It's only partially true, as the destruction of membranes leads to spinal injury, crushing of intervertebral cartilages and consequently heavy compression of the ventral parts of vertebrae, and partially crumble the periosteum and even affect the latticework of bone filling containing embryonal connective tissue and bone marrow (substantia spongiosa) according to autopsy findings of the cervical spine by Horst Weiler.

Taking into account the super sensitivity of the periosteum, it is very likely that the pain with its inevitable constant reinjury exceeds the pain of the crushing of the parotid gland.

The impact of this dens axis "attack" upon the spinal cord has not yet been explored. It might be assumed to have both long term physical consequences and painful sensations for a horse, but there is no verified data and I don't want to speak before there is proof.

Nevertheless there is probably nothing pleasant or good in any painful force, especially considering its direct impact upon the spinal cord.

However, the physiological outcomes of crushing the parotid gland, compression of vertebrae and tearing of membranes ensures invalidism and bitter death for a horse.

But as I've told you, we won't examine that now. We are solely examining the pain factor as the main "tool" of equestrian sport and its impact on a horse.

The cited findings above make it possible to affirm definitively that the pain factor is very strong, and may be exorbitant.

There is no doubt that the pain factor is the very tool by means of which sportsmen control a horse. It is clear that all so-called "sports" horses are similarly injured.

Only one thing is incomprehensible: How and why does the horse stand for such severe pain? Why, while enduring steady excruciating pain in the poll and behind the jowls, does the horse continue moving, jumping or performing passage? Is there a more severe pain that "sentences" a horse to obedience?

But again we need to receive an unambiguous reply. The reply excludes any use of "belief — disbelief". We need the facts of physical proof, not just belief.

There is such pain.

The torturous effect of the bit on a horse's mouth has already been described in great detail.

This torture has been scientifically proven by veterinary medicine. But let's ask the dead horse again. And give a fair hearing to it, this time concerning dressage.

So... this is a diastema (margo interalveolaris), the place which the bit effects. The photograph 49 shows clearly common hematomas — the results of using bits. The photos show the typical injury of the lower jaw bone periosteum where the diastema (i.e. "bars of the mouth") are. This injury is practically standard in every sport horse.

Next to the injured jawbone (upper skull) is the jawbone showing the smooth diastema of the horse who never knew a bit.

The next photo shows why the bit is placed here (see photos 48–50).

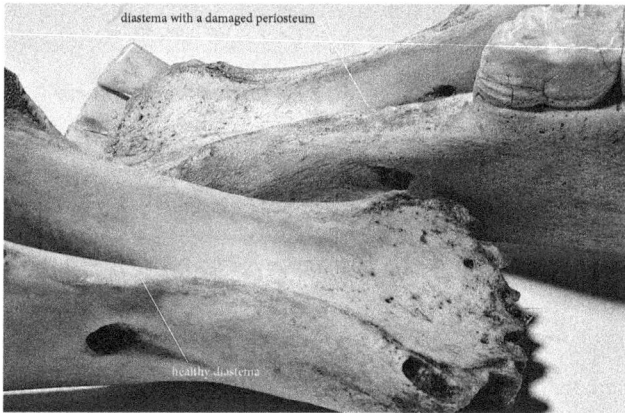
diastema with a damaged periosteum

healthy diastema

Photo 48

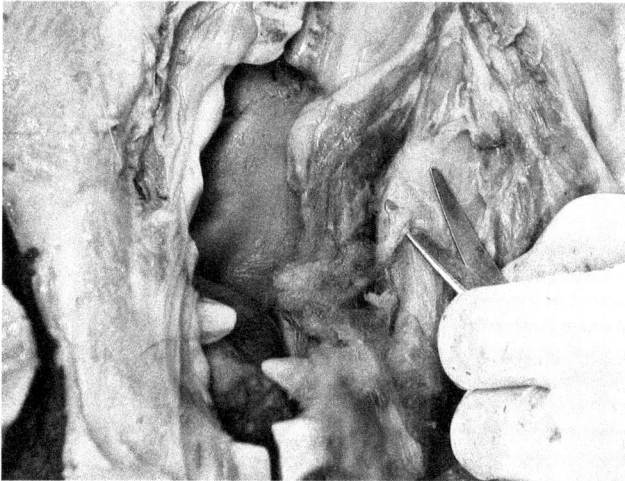
Photo 49

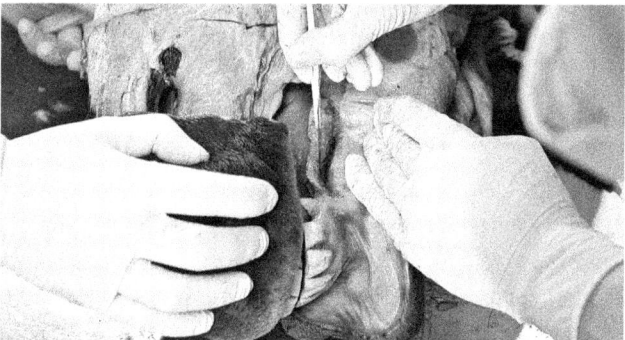
Photo 50

Here in margo interalveolaris, in diastema, the most sensitive part of trigeminal nerve is located (I am picking it up with scissors in the photo).

There is no submucosal layer on the margo interalveolaris and the bit affects the nerve directly. The nerve is supersensitive.

The bit beats and presses right on this place. What is the force of this beating and pressing?

In the course of recorded experiments it was found out that a jerk on the bit causes the press force of 300 kg per square centimeter.

An "ordinary" typical effort by so-called "good hands", is about 120-130 kg per square centimeter.

That is 120–130 kg straight to the nerve.

According to descriptive adjectives, pain like that in the area of the nerve can be called "especially acute, burning, paralyzing".

(Perhaps the "jerking" pressure is in fact much stronger. But neither the dynamometers nor other special equipment of the Forensic Medical Examination laboratory were able to measure the stronger efforts. The instruments returned an off-scale reading when the typical equestrian sport practice of "sawing the reins" and other force tensions were employed.)

All the experiments were carried out together with specialists and experts of the Forensic Medical Examination Office in St. Petersburg, veterinarians and journalists. The experiments were formally recorded and videotaped. Thus, whether one agrees with the outcomes of these experiments or not, it is really a matter of fact, not of belief.

During the course of experiments emerged the degree of traumatic pressure to the tongue of the horse.

The anatomical model of the tongue made from ballistin was practically crushed by a gentle effort from the hands of a thirteen-year-old boy (see photos 51–53).

(Ballistin is the material that most closely resembles the structure and density of living tissues in everything except flexibility. In forensic medical examination, ballistin is used to register a hit or pressure). The main pressure of the bit acts upon places where the lingual nerve (lingualis) plexus is located.

The bit causes a pressure on the tongue of 100 kg per square centimeter (this is with an ordinary rein tension; the rein acts as a connection for the bit of

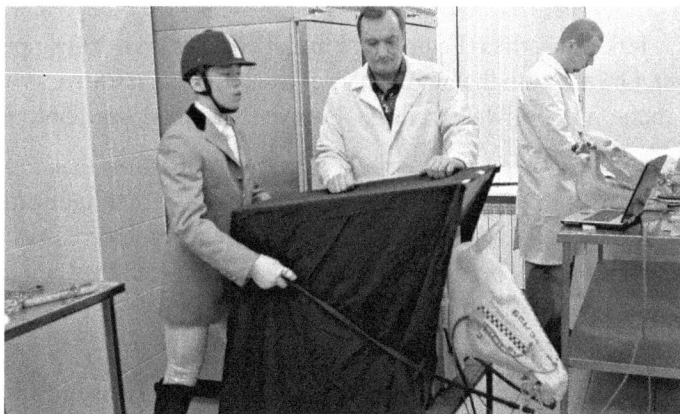
Photo 51. © Lydia Nevzorova

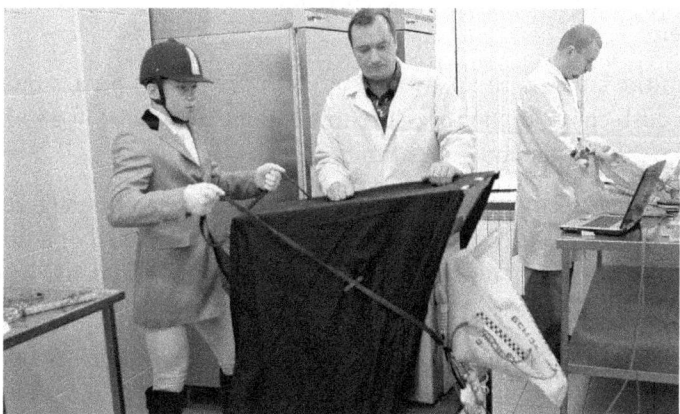
Photo 52. © Lydia Nevzorova

Photo 53. © Lydia Nevzorova

course). A jerk intensifies the pressure and it reaches 250–300 kg per square centimeter. Or rather on the lingual nerve which is supersensitive as well. (The white branch on the model is a lingual nerve (lingualis), see photo 53.)

I believe there is no need to describe the painful sensation that comes from a pressure of 200–300 kg on the sensory nerves. A real tongue would take such pressure. Owing to the super flexibility of living organic tissue, all of the more muscular tissue would reshape immediately. It would sustain an injury, but the pressure wouldn't make such a mark on it as it does on artificial ballistin. Let's continue.

Another branch of the trigeminal nerves sustains a hit. This branch is located in the chin groove under which a curb chain runs. This place is almost devoid of muscular tissue, there is only skin, a branch of nerves and periosteum there.

What can the curb chain do, a very standard curb chain on a standard curb bit? The curb chain applies pressure to the bone and nerve at an amount of more then 300 kg per square centimeter.

The force measurement instruments used to measure the degree of curb chain pressure were used in another way. A different model of a horse head was made from material withstanding the pressure of about 100 kg before it breaks with its thickness of 3 cm.

TWO EXPERTS of various ages and constitutions using two different models BROKE OFF the lower jaw after the first tensioning of the reins, which confirms the readings of the instruments.

Clearly horse bone is able to withstand much stronger pressures on this area, but we're not talking about functional damages. We are concerned with the degree of pain that a horse feels caused by the use of standard sports equipment.

Now, let us consider THE HARD PALATE (palatum durum) (see photos 54–55).

Both the curb port and the central part of the snaffle cause an equal effect on "gently rolled tissue", on the mucous membranes of palatum durum. The only difference is that pressure of the curb port is nearly constant and the hits by the central part of the snaffle are more abrupt but occasional. The thickness of masticatory mucous varies from 2 mm (within the grooves) to 6 mm (on the ridge).

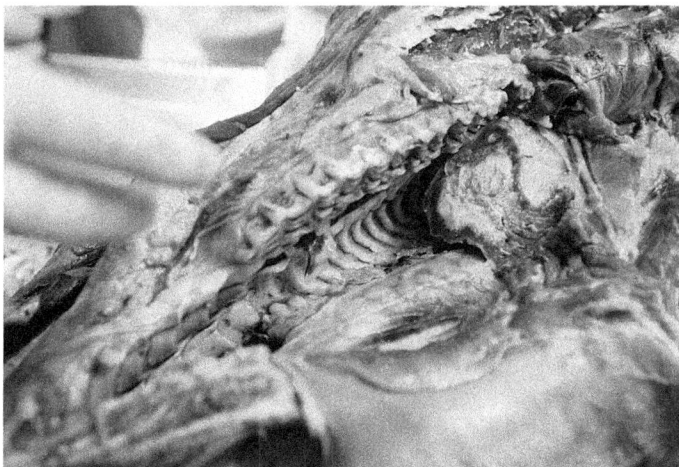

Photo 54. © Lydia Nevzorova

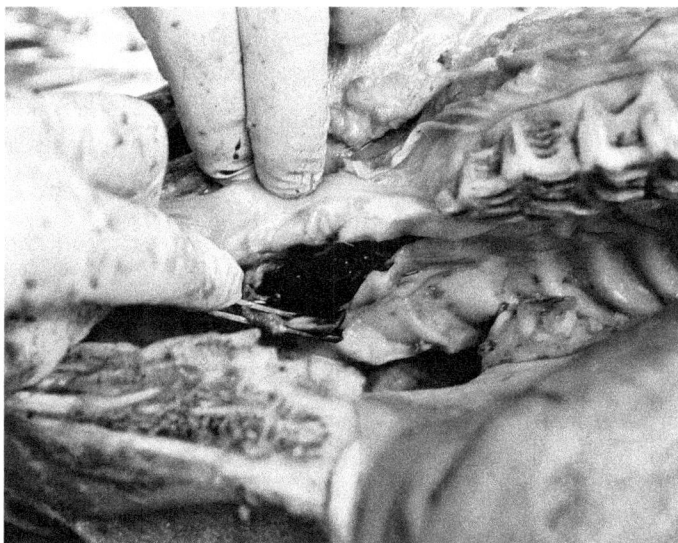

Photo 55. © Lydia Nevzorova

Between this thin layer of mucous membrane and palatine bones are located the thick branches of the palatine nerve (n. palatines major).

This thin layer of mucous membrane is unable to protect the palatine nerves against the hits and pressure of 180–200 kg per square centimeter caused by the bit.

The hematomas under the mucous membrane, which can be perfectly seen in the dissection photographs, give an idea of the amount of pressure force (and therefore the degree of pain can be inferred).

These photos show the real thickness of the hard palate mucous membrane.

We might continue talking about the impact of bits on the teeth and lips, or how they shove the horse's tongue into its throat, about the injuries to the epiglottis and so on, but much thorough research has already been dedicated to it.

Now we are talking only about the DEGREE OF PAIN, or rather about how severe that pain must be to make the horse "forget" about the pain in his poll and in the area of the parotid gland.

The performed experiments obtained figures which are easily converted to physiological sensations. These provide unequivocal evidence that pain in the mouth is more intense, sharper, or more "hypnotic", than even such severe pain as pain in the decomposing gland and crumbling vertebrae.

Therefore the horse "obeys".

The medals of Van Grunsven or Poturaeva speak volumes about that as well, though.

I have to confess when I first saw the findings of the examinations I couldn't believe my eyes. I didn't believe the experts. I didn't believe the instruments. We changed dynamometers and electronic sensors twice. But everything was repeated again and again. I didn't realize that even an ordinary "gentle" action of the bit in the mouth is so painful.

I knew that the pain exists, and that it is strong (I also used to work with bits in the past), but I was not ready for figures of 100, 200 and 300 kg per square centimeter.

It seemed to me that with an effect like that, the horse's head would fall apart during the first training. But we deal with very strong, very buoyant flesh, with very powerful physiology and a very substantial osteal system. So, 300 kg per square centimeter is not the limit yet. The head does not fall apart. It just paralyzes the horse with pain.

By the way, the experiments were also conducted on real cadaver horse heads. With the pressure of 300 kg horseflesh does not really "fall apart". Severe inner "paralyzing" injures are inflicted but there are no signs of external damage. (A real horse mandible can be fractured at the pressure of 450–600 kg. The "old School" curb-bits of S. de la Broue or D. Izvitti design ensure that effect).

Ordinary sports curb bits, or the ones that are used in classical dressage, just crack the periosteum. They can exceed the pressure of 300 kg but only just a little. The dilettante, who wants to believe in the myths of equestrian sport, cannot see the severe injuries. They are not obvious.

Veterinarians stay silent in a cowardly manner. They make a living serving sport. Ninety-nine percent of their "client base", their profits, connections, and career opportunities come from sport.

Yes, everything connected with show jumping and dressage is steady, painful torture for any horse.

Everyone who deals with a horse liberated from painful action knows that the horse with an ability to "vote", with belief that the torture is over forever, has nothing in common with the downhearted sports horse moving under the hypnosis of constant pain.

For many years sportsmen have been generating lots and lots of lies about horses. They consider the drilled, forced, obviously "painful" movements, which have nothing in common with natural biomechanics of a horse, "beautiful". They award medals to each other when the horse shows these movements. The more there is a "pain component" and marionette-like movements of a horse, the higher the mark. It is a concern for both so-called "sport" and so-called "classical" riding.

However, this again is sentimental talk. We have scientifically proven facts which dot the i's at last.

So, we can sum up and get back to the starting point of the research. People who take up so-called "dressage" are looking for some "special" feelings in it. They get them.

Every movement of the bit in the mouth, with the spurs and the whip, has a purpose and results in causing either more or less pain to a horse. This is the main irrevocable "component" of their pastime.

Do they know about the pain they cause a horse? Do they know that they are killing the horse?

Of course, you could say that about one hundred percent of dressage riders both in sport and "classical" disciplines are barbarians. Illiterate barbarians who have no idea about parotid gland structure, facial nerve branches, about the super vulnerability of the mandibular gland…. They know nothing about the horse, about his anatomy, how he moves, and what he feels.

Yes, it is so.

They are barbarians, it must be confessed at last. Nuno Oliveira, Alois Podhajsky and Guérinière were barbarians, too. All those people really had no notion of the strength and structure of the "toy" they broke for their own pleasurable sensations, self-affirmations and some "aesthetic ideals".

Arthur Kottas, the star of the School of Vienna, toured Moscow not long ago and without scruple demonstrated in public his complete ignorance about the anatomy and physiology of a horse. Needless to say this is also true about dressage riders in sport. That is to say that if they are illiterate, if they don't feel the horse, if they don't understand and don't know her anatomy and physiology, if they don't understand anything, are they mistaken when they torture a horse and think it's okay for her?

What drives them then, they who are worshiping fanatically with awe the pastime, which is based on causing severe traumas and violent pain to a living creature?

Their fanaticism is so strong that any possibility of relationship with a horse which excludes pain and death of a horse they take loathingly?!!

Alas, there is a science called psychology and it discovered everything long ago. It is known that it does not matter whether a person possesses the knowledge of what he does or not. He is aware of some feelings about what he does.

This is called sense perception, emotional knowledge.

The information, value and accuracy of this sense perception, containing dozens, even hundreds of sensations, nuances and instincts, can rival scientific knowledge.

But it differs from scientific knowledge quite fundamentally. It is impossible to express. It is difficult to formulate and to note.

But that doesn't mean it does not exist. In short, a person who ruins a horse realizes what he does. Not on a scientific level, but on an emotional level.

The possibility to force, tear and pull around the flesh, to manipulate both its deep and subcutaneous strata, to triumph over the living creature, known by the name of HORSE, methodically via pain, are probably the very feelings they look for in dressage.

Has anybody the heart to call dressage a normal pastime of sane people? But then the answer is already quite clear through the analogy with BDSM. And it is fully justified.

Everything stated above does not apply to the persons whose pictures were used to illustrate these studies.

I accept that these people could not realize the fateful consequences of their pastime on a horse.

I testify that all sportsmen in the photos acted according to all standards of behavior established in equestrian sport, and in full conformity with all guidelines of the FEI.

CRUSHING OUT: ANATOMY OF A HIPPODROME

Author:

"I knew that one day it would happen, and tried to prepare for this in my heart, studying photos from necropsies, resolutely downloading internet-photos of the most serious wounds, trying to get used to seeing blood and gore. And before this day I fondly thought that I was ready. But real life threw before my eyes things that I knew and suspected only in theory, and now my life became divided into the periods BEFORE and AFTER that photo shoot..."

Comment:

I've decided to edit this article myself and to delete nearly all of the author's emotions from it; all her hate, all her despair and all her pain, all of these extremely strong words which were born from a very natural — and very noble hatred of those who make all these activities typical and acceptable.

It was the first time, when our author saw THIS. She did not know, that THIS is absolutely normal and typical. The partial or full breaking and ripping off of a horse's leg during a race on a Russian racecourse even has its own special term. In the lingo of those fine fellows who know nothing, but ride fast horses (more often referred to as "jockeys") it is called "crushing out". Maybe there are other slangy jockeys' terms, because breaking a leg during a race is so common.

It is usually not discussed on the racecourses, in fact, it is forbidden. All the methods of keeping these facts a secret have already been rehearsed and put into practice perfectly.

Racecourse owners and jockeys understand very well that if the secret details of their activities become widely known — even children will spit in their faces,

Photo 56. © Sophia Spartantseva

Europe. Standard racecourse. The presentation of the summer horseracing season. Of course, all of these horses are very young. Of course, they're panicking. Their death has already started for them. Loving horse owners, following the strict and accepted horseracing practice, tie down the horses' tongues to the lower jaw with pieces of stockings or nylon ropes. (With this idiotic practice they prevent the horse from any chance of using tongue movement to resist the painful and paralyzing action of the bit and other specific kinds of iron.)

even those who aren't dealing with horses and their problems at all. They will spit not figuratively, in some symbolic way, but physically, with saliva, showing their hatred and contempt. Aiming right into those dull and colourless eyes shaded by the riding hat.

That's why they've created the system of canvas curtains that are immediately brought and put around the dying horse, shielding from people's eyes the elements of agony and the fatal injection of sodium thiopental and potassium chloride. That's why all the vets are being paid off, and horserace photographers will take only canonical, pristine photos for show.

There is one more detail that helps horserace riders to keep the horse's agony, the blood and torture a secret. This factor is the huge racecourse size, its remote distance from the stands making the tragedies that happen unclear and invisible to spectators.

This article can be considered valuable scientific equine material, because it has unique documenting photographs.

Of course, these photos are ruthless, but the racecourse reality, which tortures and kills thousands of horses, hypocritically smiling and shaking with prize cups and rugs, is even more ruthless.

As it was already mentioned, because of the academic commitment of the NHE publications I've seriously edited this text, leaving only several fragments that have fewer epithets and can at least be printed. Fragments of the author's text and photos I've annotated with necessary comments.

Author:

"I had already decided to leave, when I saw one last horse, galloping on the track. I've never seen such a gallop — clumsy, fast, stumbling all the time, changing leads, and when she came closer — I saw that thing, that I had seen only on pictures before that: her hind leg was broken in the area of the fetlock joint.

It was shaking in the air on each beat, and when the horse stood on this leg, she stood right on the bone."

She stood near the entrance to the paddock, the colourful, noisy crowd was running around shouting. The owner was also amongst them — it was a fat

Photo 57. © Sophia Spartantseva

Normal racecourse speeds are fatal for a horse. Her physiology "understands" this very well and will never allow such movement in natural life. Every horse has myological and physiological self-regulation laws, which always reduce the speed or even stop the horse. Even a typical racecourse speed is destructive to a horse's limbs, and also leads to exercise-induced pulmonary hemorrhage (EIPH, or "bleeding") and obstruction of breathing. But jockeys need the speed even faster than the normative one. Only this speed wins races. The beatings that a horse gets from the jockey can only partially switch off these security systems, covering their "protest" with hurt because of the painful burning beating and with horror in anticipation of the next beating. That's why sportsmen had to create a special breed, which has a reactive panic attack of such strength that it will switch off all the safety systems of the limbs, lungs and heart itself.

pig-like male who was shouting loudly to the whole racecourse. He was shouting and indignant. I was afraid to go there, where that horse was standing, where this crowd was running.

I was afraid to see that scene that I had seen a minute ago, because even that one moment was enough to make me go cold with horror. But I knew that if I don't do this now, I'd never be able to do this again. I went…

The paddock was being vacated, all the accredited photographers also left, THIS wasn't interesting for them, moreover, it was forbidden for them to take photos of this, their aim was to show the "beauty" of equine sport.

The horse wasn't allowed to go inside, somebody was holding her by the bridle. The owner, this fat pig, running to the exit, just quickly looked at what had happened, and shouting even louder, ran back, wiping his hypocritical tears from his fat cheeks, and running from everything: from his injured horse, from the responsibility and even from money.

I went to the parapet, where she was standing. I can say that she was calm, only her nostrils were rising very quickly, and her eyes were showing pain and confusion…

She still tried to step on her broken leg, maybe surprised at the strange and unknown feelings, surprised because of pain that appeared in her leg. She stepped down and raised it again. Raised for a step, and again, and again… The leg was bleeding…

Suddenly the shouts became louder. At the beginning I did not understand was happening, and after that saw that the crowd was looking at me. They looked at me with hatred and contempt, angry voices were heard. One of the stewards shouted: 'No photographing!' (I quickly understood, they had just noticed me!) waving with their hands, telling to switch off the camera and to delete the photos. He tried to catch me by the jacket, I jumped away from the parapet, that was, fortunately, high enough for the old steward not to be able to jump over it. It was also problematic for him to climb under the rails. The situation in the crowd became extremely heated, and I understood that it was time to escape.

Suddenly the piggish owner appeared, who shouted something like: 'This bitch is photographing!' Switching off the camera, I ran to the exit. On my way I looked one last time at the poor horse, said goodbye to her, and ran

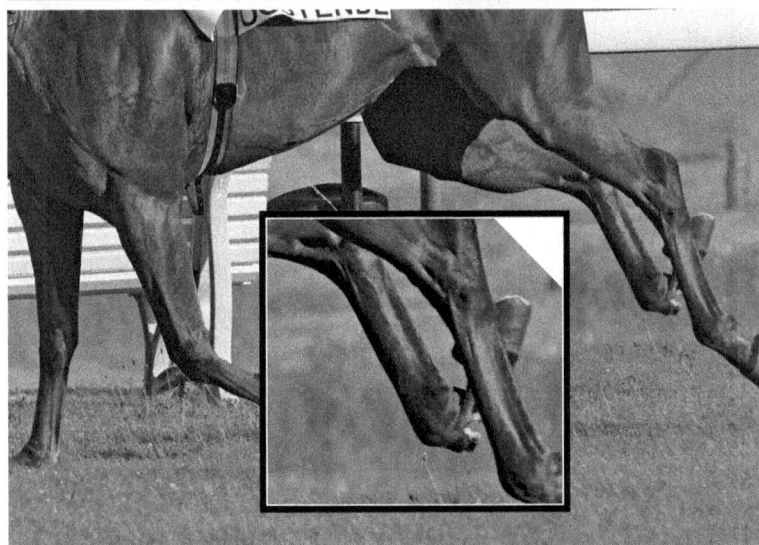

Photo 58. © Sophia Spartantseva

And suddenly the thing, which must happen, happens. This can (and must) happen because of the enormous overloading of the horse's organism due to the speed and panic, and also because of a tiny stumble. It is (in this particular case) the tearing of the hind limb, in the jockeys' slang, "crushing out". In this photo we can see the starting phase of tearing out, the partial separation of the distal epiphysis, the partial destruction of the joint. Although, here the common digital extensor tendon is already torn, the skin and the third metatarsal bone are torn as well. The lateral collateral ligament is at the stage of tearing. The bone of the first phalanx is crushed.

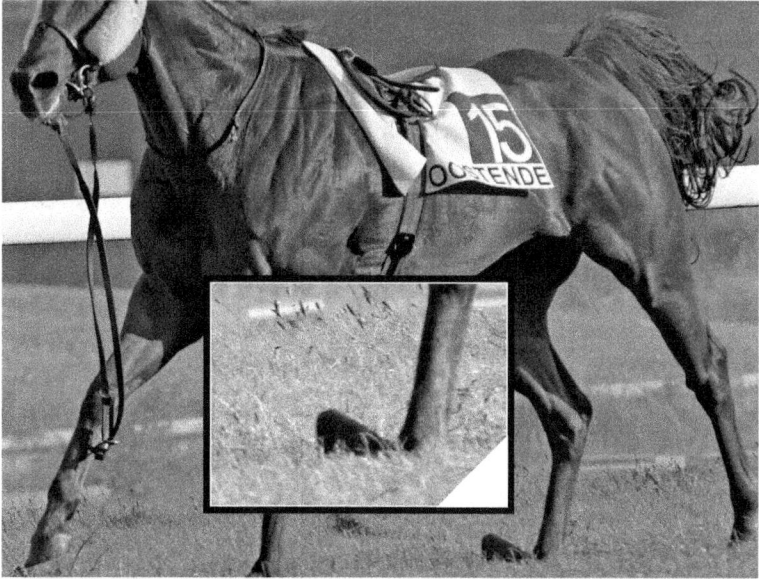

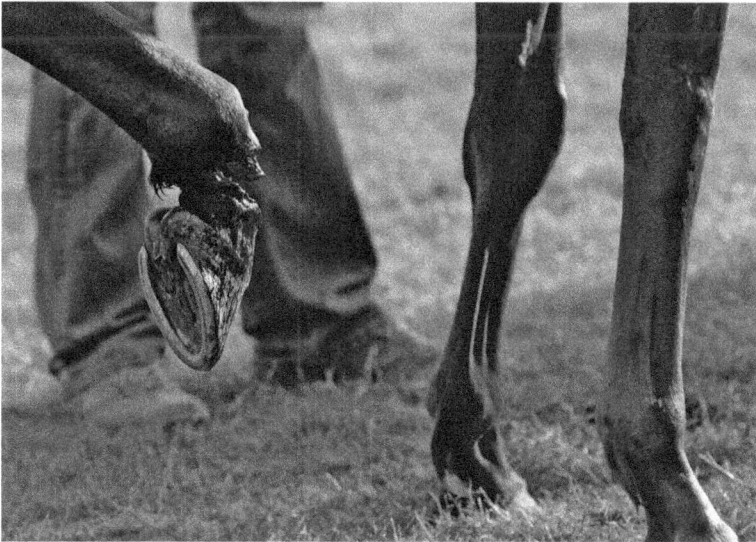

Photo 59. © Sophia Spartantseva

Here we can also see this moment quite well. Actually, in one of the gallop phases we can see the digging of the crushed first phalanx bone into the ground, and after that the phase of the full tearing of the collateral tendon begins. Here at least, we see a "good case", the tear is not full, as often happens.

The absence of the canvas curtains is a mistake that can only happen at the beginning of the racing season and only if the racecourse was repaired between the seasons. After serious repairs it is very hard to find anything.

to the side exit — it was necessary to save these photos. Only these photos can show and tell people the truth, to show the proof of the horse's torture. I knew, that if I stayed one more minute, they'd contact the guards and they would stop me. Jumping into a narrow corridor, I tried to take out the battery and memory card, and suddenly realized that I didn't know how to do this! I hadn't learned yet. But I had to do something. Putting the camera into my bag, I went straight to the exit. I was surprised when I saw that the man, who was standing near the entrance a minute ago, was gone now, the racecourse gates were left unattended.".

Comment:

In such cases the injured horse is usually killed right on the field. The actual method of euthanasia varies from racecourse to racecourse. Sometimes the horse is killed by an anesthetic dose of sodium thiopental followed immediately by a fatal dose of potassium chloride.

Sometimes simply by a "knock-down" overdose of sodium thiopental, that is injected not drop by drop, but in a rapid stream. If potassium chloride is ever used without sodium thiopental it results in very long and painful agony, that is all too apparent.

Author:

"I didn't want to go home, didn't want to do anything. The most horrible thing was to be alone, together with the last thoughts and the last-seen scenes, which were still in front of my eyes. I decided to go to the train station to meet my husband.

On my way I started to understand that a long time must pass before I decide to look at these photos again. My husband promised to put them into the computer and to save them in a folder that only he knew of, and to send them to the magazine. 'Tell me when you feel OK, I'll show you where they are.' he said.

…I'll never forget this horse and will do everything I can to avenge her. Maybe the entrance to the racecourse is blocked for me now — they'll remember my face. But that's not important.

Their thinly covered secrets have already been taken away from the pain-etched walls, behind which other horses still stay. These bastards will get '...' (Deleted by me, AN). And now... let's wish green fields for the small chestnut horse, where she doesn't feel pain anymore..."

Sophya Spartantseva
All photos by **Sophya Spartantseva**

Comments by **Alexander Nevzorov**

COLLECTION: DEAD OR ALIVE

The Russian Federation is deaf when it comes to horses.

The scandal that has recently shocked the horse world in Europe and America remains absolutely unknown of here.

When the the news broke, it seemed that its terrible and great theme described by the main editor of the German magazine "ST.GEORG", Gabriella Pochhammer, would turn the European and American equestrian circles upside down.

The upshot of the story was that the most authoritative trainers, journalists, judges and veterinarians are aware that methods of horse training used for sport dressage are excruciating for horses. Everything erupted.

The Olympic champions' medals are tarnished, their colour diminished from golden to dirty and bloody. The sponsors, who financed the competitions, thought about what they had been supporting and stopped funding.

Suddenly it has emerged that even in sporting Europe — hundreds of specialists were aware of the painful nature of the horse training system and what is more, they were ready to speak about it openly.

And they began speaking.

The authoritative trainer Klaus Balkenhol has based his reasonings on the findings of German veterinarians. He frankly confirms on the pages of "ST. GEORG" that the execution of all modern dressage causes permanent pain.

In Aachen (2004) the judge Kristof Gess, whilst observing training by the aspirants for the gold medals, made two cessations for blatant cruelty.

In one case the audience witnessed Nadine Capellmann's sorrel gelding Elvis revolt. He took off running in stead of doing piaffe. The explanation was that he had a pinched sciatic nerve, but everyone understood what it was really about.

In Las Vegas an audience demanded the intervention in the training of the Olympic champion Anky Van Grunsven. The judge gave her a warning for cruel methods.

When Judge Vitkhages frankly acknowledges, "This training requires the interference of veterinarians." He is referring to the methods of Olympians.

In Bielefeld the German prosecutor's office has already begun a court case against J.Berndt and H.Jurgen, trainers in sport dressage. The "New Westphalian Agency" in Bielefeld reported: "During the process of teaching piaffe the horse was cruelly beaten and, covered in blood, fell in the stable passage way. The whips used for the beating were confiscated and forensic testing proved the presence of the blood of many horses on them…"

When the scandal erupted, the term "sadism" was practically on every page of "ST. GEORG", and Gabriella Pochhammer began playing with fire.

The letters of the magazine's readers were published in abundance. For example, this is a letter from Silvia Kruschke-Schaht from Lupendorf: "You stand near a riding hall and feel ashamed that you haven't got enough courage to set a note of infamy to the sadism".

At the center of the scandal was the Olympic champion, Anky Van Grunsven, the grim demon with her cruel method of collection, called rollkur.

The legality and honesty of Anky's medals became doubtful. Naturally, the question arose about the need to reconsider the Olympian's results.

And it was understood that if this situation was to follow its logical course, it would also be necessary to dismiss all the FEI leaders; to disqualify 99 percent of the worlds leading sportsmen; to dismiss the FEI veterinarians. Moreover, the whole system of refereeing in sport dressage (which even previously was very questionable and loose) after such a strong blow as this, would be dismissed.

The Viennese horse-breakers (as well as the Saumur, the Brussel's Academy, and the School of Baron Neidorf, along with their legitimate mental children

Photo 60. © Sophia Spartantseva

of endless Oliveiras, Karls, Henrikets and their bastards as well) alertly observed the scandal as they knew that they also had their faces in the trough.

Obsessed with trying to maintain civility, Europe realized that publicity of the truth about horse training methods for equestrian sport would destroy not only the sport but also the so-called "classics", which are related to sport and are sympathetic with its sporting methods. Indifference to the scandal came only from the Royal Andalusian School and the Portuguese. In these countries where cow killing is turned into public fun as a norm, where the public knows perfectly well that bullfighting kills 1500 to 2500 bulls every year, but continues to apotheosize this cretin entertainment, the horse tormentors have nothing to worry about. But the Spanish and the Portuguese, who, due to bullfighting, manage to emulate the image of a living pithecanthropus, make no weather in Europe.

Every scandal participant, when made aware of the consequences of this conflict and the understanding that the veterinary moral-fire could destroy both sports and classical dressage, have come to their senses and rushed to douse it. By the way, the beauty Gabriella Pochhammer, the firebrand and the incendiary, was one of the first.

The veterinary research suffocated under the asses of "FEI specialists" who sat heavily on the topic. Toothless disputes and sweet politically-correct conferences brought down the huge problem which had "suddenly" appeared.

The court case of Anky Van Grunsven against "ST.GEORG" had announced a decision which satisfied them all. As it was, the court did not consider the veterinary part of the question, and considered only the harm to Anky's honor.

As a result, the magazine, with its accusations, has appeared as not guilty, and Anky appeared innocent too, because she "has worked according to the norms of horse sports".

Of course, the condemnation of the norms of horse sports was not and could not be included into the competence of the court.

The scandal was over. Done away with. Disappeared.

The followers of equine sports and equine "classics" have relaxed with a deep breath, wrongly supposing that the worst is over.

They haven't understood that people and times have changed.

They have not understood that the nasty Anky incident was only one of the first signs in the revaluation, changes in the tectonic placement in history between the relationship of the man and horse.

And they can't even imagine what will follow.

Refreshing our minds about the scandal hasn't been that necessary, but it will help in the research of the most important question to which this article is devoted.

The scandal prompted German and American veterinarians to begin detailed exploration of the horses' neck for the first time. (It is true that the enormous cruelty of the training and electric shockers, villainous with its cruel method of control, have remained outside the scandal, because they were not proven. And nobody even tried to prove it, because the magazine staff thought that the Germans were unprepared for this. But you cannot hide an awl in a sack, and some methods have nevertheless became known; for example, forcing a horse to raise up its legs with the help of special gear that dooms the horse to arthritis and arthrosis. But all of these are non-things and particularities.)

So, the reason for the initial situation, which almost nullified dressage as an Olympic discipline, was the so-called collection used by Anky Van Grunsven, the method that is called rollkur.

Rollkur in its essence is a very overdone collection, done in utmost secrecy it is very severe and strict. My colleague, Professor Robert Cook characterizes it as "false collection, practically paralyzing the horse's back and assisting the development of unnatural constrained movements". It is these movements which are considered by sportsmen of all riding levels as "perfect" and are highly marked by the judges.

The fact that at the base of these movements lies a pathology, the distortion of horse biomechanics and definite torture, is hardly understood by anyone and is interesting for only a few people. These movements are extracted from the horse by the use of force, and because the training is based exclusively on pain, such as rollkur, also serve as a fundamental guard against revolt. But, honestly, this aspect is additional. The main function of rollkur is the blocking of the horse's back and entire top line and as a result causes severe limitation of sight which leads to blindness and the stretching or breaking of the intervertebral cartilages of the cervical spine.

Deformation of the cervical spondylus is clearly visible in these photos — the result of collection methods used by equestrian sports. I repeat again: these vertebras are not after rollkur, but after common dressage collection. Rollkur, the Olympic collection, deforms them even more severely.

Relying on the known facts about blindness caused by rollkur, we can now talk about the horse's sensations (For informational purposes for vets: you can get acquainted with detailed consequences of rollkur and common collection by looking through works by autopsist Horst Weiler. They are available).

Opinions of authoritative veterinarians are the same: rollkur leads to absolute and specific destruction of the cervical and lumbar spine. The consequences are tragic. Nevertheless, rollkur is the ultimate of forced collection in equestrian sports, it is the model (judging by the number of glossy ribbons on necks of Van Grunsven, Isabell Werth, Nadine Capellmann and other dressage-queens). Any rider who wants to have high scores in international competitions must doom his horse to rollkur. In the veterinarians' opinion rollkur cripples a horse, but it brings Olympic gold. For those who want to be successful in dressage, rollkur is unavoidable.

But why am I telling you all this? It is clear that equestrian sport attracts only the people who cannot empathize with the horse — otherwise they wouldn't do it. What else can we expect to see from them, the sportsmen, taking into account their phenomenal platitude and absence of feeling for a horse?

It must be said, that it is a big mistake to think that rollkur is a sports invention. Rollkur is an invention of classical dressage. Engravings of that era clearly represent it.

Actually, it is absolutely unscientific to base serious opinions on those engravings or paintings.

It would be better to examine the style of the heirs of classical schools: Louise Valence, the Peralta brothers, Nuno Oliveira, Luraschi and his School. The same thing is seen everywhere.

We can examine the work, as you may have already guessed due to the colours of the poitrel on the black horse — of the Royal Andalusian School of Riding. Everywhere here we see the epitome of hard, painful, forced, pulled flexion and the forced, painful bringing of the hind limbs under the body.

Practically the same business is in the Viennese and Saumur Schools as well as by Bartabas, Bragants, Kate Enrike. The classics just don't call it rollkur, however, it is simply the utmost of cruel false-collection that has the same purpose as rollkur. It has exactly the same mechanism for its execution.

It looks a little different. Yes! In a dilettante's judgment, the flexion line of the occiput and neck somehow differs. But this is explained by the fact that the Iberian, Andalusian, Lipizian and Lusitano horses (used in so-called "classics") have a neck that makes resentment to collection a bit more effective than other "liquidneckers" or warm-blooded (if to compare to the Andalusians) breeds of Europe.

The scene, but only the scene, is a bit different. The essence remains the same. Absolute cruelty in the process of attaining vertical flexion, that from time to time turns into severe flexions between the third and fourth cervical vertebras.

In the so-called "classics", as in sports, is the use of special tools which produce a forced, reflectory affected, marionette-like kind of movement.

Because this style is unnatural and absolutely harmful, the horse is kept in the very posture that makes any antagonism impossible. In fact, the horse is paralyzed by pain no differently than in sports.

So, either in sports or in the "classics" collection is the goal, the passion and the desire. Hundreds of gadgets, methods and maneuvers are created for attaining collection, which has a lot of different names (in French it's "rassemble"; in Russian, "сбор" (sbor)).

All right! It seems that all this should serve a very good purpose. Collection is a magical thing! To collect a horse is to mobilize him. To give him an opportunity to feel his power, to give him a feeling of a hundredfold increase of his own strength and tonus due to putting most of the force into the power of his croup and hips, due to the increase of back power — is a very logical and correct goal. Sportsmen and representatives of the "classics" desire collection for pious purposes. From that point of view, it is understandable.

They want to encourage the mount to become similar to the free, fighting, dizzy with love, energetic horse, similar to a horse that we see in a natural state, in his relative environment, in those moments of anger, fight or flirting.

The photos by Robert Vavra, the most famous horse photographer, who had practically been living in a herd of wild horses of the Camargue and Andalusia for several years show natural collection which is "turned on" by a horse when it is needed.

All this is the truth. The power of a horse grows greatly.

Nature has given a horse an immense biomechanism, which incredibly raises its power potential. All that is necessary is to have this mechanism launched and then a horse will be capable of miracles.

This is where it begins to get very interesting. A horse taught any sort of collection, no matter how it is classified: rollkur or a classical rassemble, under the action of the iron in its mouth and on its sides, really can show something similar to what free horses will show at moments of happiness or passion. But as soon as the forced influence disappears, the so-called "collection" also disappears, the back sags and the head rises.

Whatever is required from a horse, even the most difficult of tasks, the horse is ready to implement them, ugly and strained — but it never returns into collection.

Practically everyone has faced this situation. As soon as a horse receives a tiny opportunity not to be in so called collection (apprentice rider, change of bit, absence of gourmette or a smaller length of whip — I do not speak about a free horse), the horse abandons collection and the performance of any elements becomes impossible. This simple and mysterious, genius mechanism, which generates such energy, posture and power, turns off.

It is a puzzle, isn't it?

A horse naturally understands the huge advantages which are given to him by collection, he knows these very well it seems.

He already knows the feeling of his own multiplied power. Horses know that only this position — with hind legs more under hindquarters, vertical flexion, a gently tensed back — provides possibility to cope with any task. But as soon as the painful influence of the bridle and spurs stop, the horse decides not to turn this mechanism on. If we try to force a horse to do any element, it will either not execute it, or it will execute it monstrously, but it will not go into collection. Not into that collection that is seemingly so well known by a horse. This is true even of the wild horse and is incorporated into every horse without exception. Moreover, a horse which was trained to collection in one of the classical schools, had collection introduced with help of special gear.

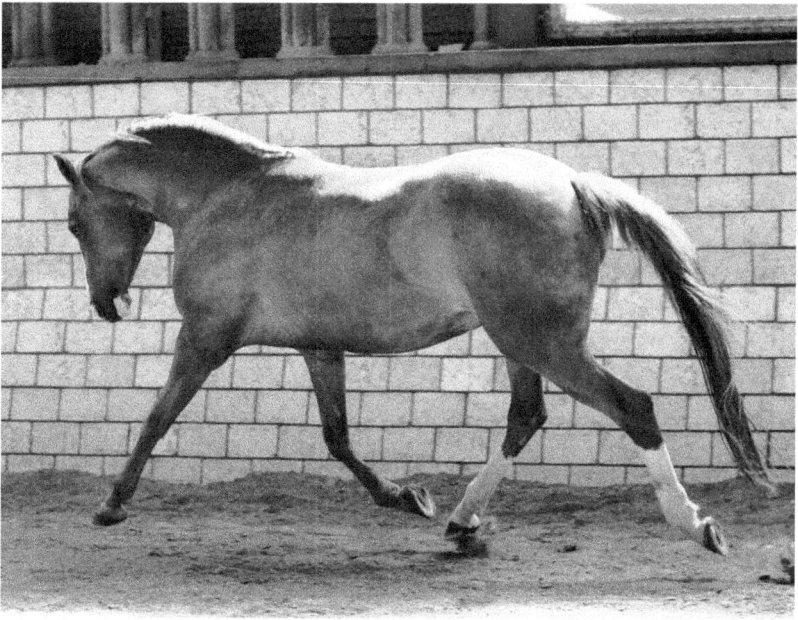

Photo 61. Lipisina and Perst in natural collection. © Lydia Nevzorova

Notice, that here the puzzle gets more complicated.

This is a simple and understandable example, everyone. I ask my assistant to hammer a nail. A typical nail. Here is the nail, hammer and wood. But although he is familiar with such an object as a hammer and has used one before, he begins to drive the nail by his palm, legs, fists, fingers etc, wounding them to blood, but he does not take the hammer, which is lying beside him! Amazing! What terrible sensations could be connected by my assistant to the hammer that he should refuse to use it, injure himself, not fulfill the task and do everything so as not to feel the hammer in his hand?

I've been thinking about this for a long time. Why does the horse throw away all the advantages of collection as soon as bit and spurs disappear?

Then I remembered that exactly the same thing had happened in my own life.

When I was very young and foolish, I turned on the ironing device that stood in my bathroom near my bath. It was an old-style Soviet iron that needed a long time to warm up, so I decided to take a bath. When I realized it was time to iron, I didn't want to leave the bath. As I did not understand physics well, I decided to iron with an electrical iron while taking the bath and so I grabbed the iron handle... Shaking captured me for a very long time. A long, scary time.

Everybody who has had such an accident knows that you can't let go of the electricity source.

Even now, years later, when I grab an iron handle I begin to shake a little. My muscles and nerves remember everything. A thousand times easier than that first time, but enough for me to avoid ironing at all.

Seemingly, the same thing happens to horses. Once it has experienced forced collection, it gets such an intense pain sensation of immense duration that it simply doesn't want to return to it on a compulsory basis. Never.

It's very simple.

How is this collection reached?

By causing pain in the jaws, the neck and the back.

How is it maintained?

By causing pain in the jaws, the neck and the back.

(If we take away all the hypocrisy, emotions and ceremonies, this is the answer we get.)

Does this pain get "remembered" by a horse?

When you look at the deformed cervical vertebras, you have to acknowledge that the pain must have been of an unbearable nature, the horse must have remembered it — certainly on a cellular level the way human cells remember trauma. Obviously, coming back to this position voluntarily, when this pain undoubtedly gets "remembered", isn't something any single sane horse would desire.

Veterinarians stay quiet on this topic or honestly answer: "the question hasn't been researched".

On the other hand, however strange it may sound, human medicine gives an answer. Studied some time ago and already a topic for hundreds of books, is post-traumatic reflection. This is when muscles and nerves "remember" severe pain and when a situation analogous to the one that caused the initial pain, begin to "remember" it again. The organism does everything in order to avoid the repetition of a situation like that.

Remember the deformation of cervical vertebras of a horse that is in forced collection.

Now we can form a clear picture of how severe the pain is for a horse in artificial collection, the collection, duration and amount of which is controlled not by the horse, but forced by man and his equipment.

The essence of the matter is that rollkur by Van Grunsven, or rassamble by Luraschi, or collection of Baucher are not, in fact, collection. They have nothing in common with collection in its real, natural incarnation.

My colleague, Professor Cook, before me, knowing nothing about my research in this area and about my practice, gathered his courage and classified all of this by a term called false collection.

I shall explain.

What is considered to be collection in sports and "classics" is a simple parametric shortening of the horse frame. Primitive (through pressure on the mouth) vertical flexion of the occiput and bringing of the croup further under the body by pain inflicted from the spur. The neck is bent at the poll through pain in the mouth, and the hind legs are stepping further under the body by the painful effect of spurs. The horse's length actually does get shorter under the effect of these factors. But these two ingredients are barely connected to each other. They are not bound into a single whole. Pain factor at the front. Pain factor from behind. Combined suffering, a state of half-blindness that lasts as long as the rider or trainer desires it to. Though there is a parametric shortening and the appearance of collection, as we already know, as soon as you remove the bit from horse's mouth, collection disappears — the horse "falls apart".

Therefore, what we see in sports and in "classics" is not collection, the state of utmost power and comfort, the athletic inspiration of the entire biological body of a horse.

Certainly, Professor Cook was correct in naming it false collection and saying it is a slow and torturous killing of a horse.

As a practitioner I can say one more thing: there are no hands so ingenious in the world that they could precisely define the duration or degree of the collection during different gaits and elements. Horse riding and skillful work with a horse in general, where movements of a horse should correspond to the desire of man, collapse before our eyes.

The story with van Grunsven, as I have said, was just one of the first signs. However, the appearance of this sign is common. It becomes wide spread as more and more people realize that there are no "relationships" between man and horse, that these are sweet fairy-tales for idiots. There is no unification, no harmony. There is only a set of severe tools which has been polished up by centuries and which are used by man to force a particular movement and behavior of horses through severe pain in the lower jaw, in the poll and the neck. It becomes more difficult to conceal the truth about the sadism and primitive essence of dressage.

There is a simple question: why should the movements of a horse look as Fillis, Baucher, Guérinière, Viennese Riding School or the FEI imagines them?

It is by the hand of all of these that force a horse to move and perform dressage elements and figures and the primary motivator for performing these elements is by the use of pain. They use it today too. (It is about the FEI and about Viennese Riding School also.) And what we see now in sports and classical dressage is the first of all the consequences of such powerful pain impacts, as this is what helps a man to control the movements and behavior of a horse. And it is a typical tendency for BASSE ÉCOLE (Low School) to fasten its ideals in passage, piaffe, courbettes and other elements and movements. Therefore, it is absolutely not allowed to speak about the naturalness of such movements, about their sincerity and freedom. Moreover, it is pain that is used as a chisel to sculpt from the natural block of horse biomechanics some sort of figure that conforms to man's vision of beauty. Besides, these perceptions of what is beautiful change depending on the epoch, or tendency in human art, or from national traditions and for many other reasons. There is one vision in Spanish dressage, another one at Chikosh, a third in Luraschis' School, a fourth at the Olympics and so on.

Why not ask a horse how it sees the performance of this or that element? In essence, all (or practically all) movements of High School are movements that are typical of games and entertainments and fights of horses in their natural habitat. Neither courbette or piaffe, nor capriole were invented by man. As I have already said, these are natural movements of the horse. Man only brings correctives into these movements by deforming them with pain to suit his own vision of beauty and ideals.

For some, these things seem normal. For me it is disgusting. I'm not interested in the standards and rules of classical dressage and I don't care that piaffes and terre-a-terres of my horses don't always fit in the classical canons.

Well what are the elements of classical dressage?

They have at least three constituents:

1) Natural biomechanical capabilities of a horse.

2) Representation of a movement that the horse makes as a result of its education by man, who asks the horse to execute a particular, natural movement, one that horses often demonstrate during courting or a fight.

3) Component of force, which the man brings in through the influence of pain through a bit in the mouth and the pain influence of spurs. This pain factor is a very strong one, and denying it is the top of dilettetantism, but it is this factor that formed the classical viewpoint on collection and elements.

So, we see this three-component list. I remove the pain component and get an element in a way that is the most comfortable for a horse to do for itself. Of course, that is why we can't compare elements performed in pain or with pain with ones that are performed absolutely without.

As I already said, the escalation in the use of painful influences, such as those used by sport dressage, is a serious problem. Olympic champions use the method of bringing pain to nerves of the head and neck that is in the extreme, as in rollkur, which is just one display of this disgusting tendency. The effect of the pain component already eclipses the natural biomechanics and art of education of a horse. To what limit it can go is unclear. The ruthlessness shown to horses in sports is progressing.

The higher degrees of this ruthlessness cause new standards and results at the Olympics. It doesn't matter to what heights the painful influences of dressage could reach, it is certain that the painful way is a dead-end one.

I do not see the point in going this way, and I do not reserve the right to cause pain to a horse for myself.

Teaching a horse passage, piaffe, capriole, courbettes, pesades etc. without any means of compulsion and pain, without "metal" bridles or halters is in my understanding of the true Haute École, i.e. the highest art in essence of work with a horse.

To a normal person who understands biomechanics, physiology and horse anatomy, as well as with veterinary science, the degree of pain caused is absolutely clear and cannot be argued. Some people are still successfully hiding from this simple knowledge, but hiding forever will not work. Scandals, judges, magazine disclosures in Germany and Holland of Van Grunsven and other Olympians are the first, yet humble jolts which predestine the inevitability of a big earthquake that will turn the horse world upside down. Humans have begun to dream about so-called relationships and friendship between man and horse – who until then, had only the skill of application of forceful gear to this astonishing creature, this creature that is capable of true friendship and love. The human ponders. It has already happened. There is no turning back. Even the most superficial knowledge of the history of the world proves that the outcome of musings like this will turn the horse world upside-down.

For this reason I began to teach my horses and then the horses of my students to perform an ALIVE and naturally free collection. This had practical necessity at first. I had been taught long, valuable and very detailed classical dressage, its techniques and figures.

Taking "metal", bridle or halter for horse control I perceive for myself as absolutely unacceptable, a savage business, as I know in detail the impact of the bit on the horse's mouth.

But! The elements of the most fabulous and always developing school of Haute École require collection. Without collection they are impossible. It is precisely these elements (passage, piaffe, cadrans, caracole and courbette) which reveal the talent of the horse and its spirit. All these movements are installed in her by nature. Moreover, teaching these elements is the best and easiest way to build correct relations with any horse, to get its respect and attention. Without collection, mounted or from the ground, they are impossible. But collection seems impossible without a bridle or halter.

This is the task I had in front of me. I solved it. The solution is described in detail in the book "The Horse Crucified and Risen". It is described honestly and precisely. Well, I just don't make a secret of the main aspect of my School.

Free collection which I teach the horse is amazingly varied in different elements. Of course, without force, if the horse feels the smallest discomfort she can release herself. Yet, astonishingly, she engages it again and uses it as an instrument for solving a difficult task. It is easy to see, by looking at photos carefully.

Here's a simple example (photo 62). The collection on the Spanish Walk is distinguished by a particular position of the head: the nuchal ligament and the rectis capitis ventralis give the neck a sort of crested position. The occiput clearly reads every half-tempo of the shoulders as they rise, turning into a point of amortization that at once restores equilibrium with its nodding, when there is the need to begin moving his left leg, while the movement of his right leg is not yet finished.

Perhaps you remember the saying about men who undress women with their eyes, in the mind taking off their clothes. So then, the one who wants to do High School seriously, should do the same with a horse, i.e. he should get his vision under the horse's skin, noticing and clearly imagining the work of all muscles, joints and bones. I want to remind my students once more that development of this "myological vision" is a categorical necessity.

Photo 62. © Lydia Nevzorova

Photo 63. © Lydia Nevzorova

Photo 64. © Lydia Nevzorova

Photo 65. © Lydia Nevzorova

Photo 66 a–b. © Lydia Nevzorova

Photo 67, 68. © Lydia Nevzorova

And this "myological vision" can only be based on a perfect knowledge of horse anatomy and understanding of its biomechanics.

Let's return to the Spanish Walk. Despite the simplicity of this element, it is very demonstrative. Certainly, if there was a bit in the horse's mouth and the head was cramped by reins, if collection was defined by man, a horse would suffer damage to both the cervical vertebras and ligaments.

The collection during standing is absolutely different. It is much freer, with seemingly bigger neck flexion, muscles of the croup and hips are virtually switched off, but in concentration are the extensors of the forward legs, weight of the neck is inverted and slanting into the shoulders. But right here, in the shoulders, the effort dissolves, it disappears, and the muscles of the shoulders are at marvelous rest (photo 63).

The third picture is piaffe and a third variation of collection. Absolute equilibrium of a horse is achieved here by glimmering collection. Again, the occiput very sensitively picks up all the diagonal oscillations and finds the point where this lifting is the most effective (photo 64–65).

In passage — the fourth collection. It is already different in principle than piaffe, with seemingly solo work of biceps femoris, quadriceps femoris and muscles the of hips and croup — all are seriously loading the neck muscle apparatus. And especially clear – the trapezius muscle. The passage collection of a free horse defines and pumps up the trapizius muscle, while artificial collection causes well known consequences when trapezius muscles — in both cervical and thoracic parts — are in full atrophy. A collapse forms near the withers that can be seen from a distance of 100 meters.

Again, the conflict between natural biomechanics and dead collection — false collection — is obvious. And on a cadran (that is to say a pirouette) — the fifth collection is much freer and open, because the horse very precisely balances itself, creating an amazing mix of vertical and lateral flexions.

The bit, reins and the hands force an absolutely different frame on a horse during a pirouette, which as it has come to be known, is hostile to the horse's natural biomechanics.

Differences of the collection in different elements are amazing. It can be observed on the given illustrations.

It is nearly guaranteed that a bit and hands would have forced the horse to carry out all elements with an identical position of the head and neck.

Controlled by man's hand the variations of strengthening-relaxing the vertical and lateral flexions, along with the forcing of the hind legs under the body in such a way that is not required by the horse, without doubt causes discomfort, pain and absence of balance compensations (due to the coruscant poll oscillation and the action of the biceps femoris muscle). Thankfully a horse free to engage itself apportions the weight and the stress from the left or the right half of the croup.

Moreover, as I have already noticed, it doesn't do it with CADENCY, but with the lightest advance for each tempo.

Indeed, the horse knows better.

To limit this genius, this absolutely perfect biomechanism, is pure nonsense. This is in essence what both classical and sports dressage do.

And I… I don't do anything supernatural. Nothing special.

You can say that I only follow the sacred tradition of Haute École and words of the grand Master of the School, Antoine de Pluvinel that were vocalized in the XVII century and that fortunately for me and my horses I understood literally:

"The largest complexity for the horse is to perform a pirouette, and the largest discomfort is inflicted by a bridle. A horse more willingly suffers the man on her back, than the bit in her mouth".

RODEO: INTIMATE DETAILS OF A NATIONAL SHAME

Rodeo exists in America. In that country it is known as a FUN NATIONAL PAS-TIME. Moreover, rodeo has become romanticized. In order to make it appear so, big money is regularly put into it.

Organizers of rodeos are delaying as long as possible the moment of explosion. Once all the details of the truth are known they understand that what they sit on is like a keg of gunpowder that will one day blow apart. The real truth about the nature of rodeo is so horrible, that a civilized world could never continue it after the truth becomes common knowledge. This knowledge will be a treasure to humanity. But the keg will explode, and it will happen very soon. It is impossible to hide the truth about the horrible and ignorant dark side of rodeo forever.

This article gives a brief description of the basic principles of rodeo; these are principles that organizers love to hide.

Of course, we apologize to the readers for this ruthlessness, but sometimes pure and accurate facts are stronger than any journalistic tricks and work better than any "expressions of feelings".

RODEO

When talking about rodeo we can only be surprised at how shameless the fairy tales are about this horrible activity. In bullfighting there is a least some semblance of an operatic storyline explaining the sequence of events, although the horse is ill-fated from the beginning. Rodeo is just a typical and primitive way for absolute idiots to have fun. Even the word idiot sounds a bit complementary towards these guys in hats and the audience who watch the rodeo.

Rodeo and bullfighting are very, very similar. Both events share that "naked zoology", when the true nature of a creature who claims its "unique origin" so loudly is bared.

The idea of bullfighting is to watch death and torture. Maybe it is an atavism that came to the XXI century from the "homo erectus", when the torture and death of a living creature, pierced with spears before the cavemen's eyes was associated with the food supply, and that's why the spectacle is so "pleasurable" for the spectators. OK, so bullfight spectators have some excuse: the past cave life of humanity, poverty and famine, the public murder of the cow and the horse as a symbol of the coming food. Spectators, remembering the ancient tales, applaud and shout happily, watching from under their low hairy brows.

Rodeo spectators do not even have this simple "scientific" reason. The death of the horse does not happen very often in front of the rodeo spectators. Of course, it happens, but much more rarely than in bullfighting.

At rodeos people just come to watch torture. To be made happy from torture, to laugh at torture. This is not even a caveman scenario. It is something worse. If we get rid of all unnecessary words, the idea of rodeo can be expressed in this manner.

Let's look at the classical variant, the bucking bronco. The aim of the cowboy is to hold onto a horse as long as possible, during his "furious jumps". The cowboy has in his arsenal horrible sharp spurs, with which he beats the horse on the neck and shoulders, but it's not these spurs that make the horse so "furious".

In reality there are no wild horses in rodeo and there is nearly no chance that there will be. There are simply old horses who are on their way to the meat factory. Rodeo is like some detour before death to them. We can joke about the horse's "swan song".

There, horses are bucking because of one… no, because of two reasons.

In 99 percent of cases they work together. They are — the flank strap and the electric prod. The flank strap is just a rope that is tied up in the area of the fifth vertebrae of the lumbar part of the vertebral column and (because most horses in rodeo are stallions and geldings) goes over the place where the penis lies.

The prod — is an electric shock device, a simple, painful electric shocker, without which rodeo is impossible. An electric jolt guarantees the "sudden" leap out of the box that rodeo fans and crowds like so much. There are different types of electric prods.

The most important thing is the strap.

The pulling of the strap takes place in two phases. First of all a cowboy in the box pulls it tightly and knots it. Then, after the horse is hit with an electric shock, the strap is pulled up as hard as possible.

After that the horse, crazy from the acute pain in a most delicate place, rushes out of the box and tries to get rid of that which presses on his waist and penis. Instinctive kicks with the hind legs, jumps and furious rushing — everything is guaranteed for the "cowboy". It does not make any difference to the cowboy. The horse is just a piece of meat here, the same as in bullfighting.

White-hatted, tobacco chewing "cowboys", who have typically killed many hundreds of horses — usually also enjoy taking photos of themselves with horses and telling everybody how they love them. Usually they use the same words as equine sportsmen. It is important to understand, that there are NO OTHER ways to make a crazy wild mustang from a quiet, sick horse, except by pulling the strap, crushing his penis and hitting him with an electric shock. It doesn't matter what anyone says — other ways DO NOT EXIST.

MEXICO

Speaking about rodeo as a cultural and national phenomenon of the USA with its cruelty and savagery towards horses, we absolutely unfairly haven't paid attention to another branch of this entertainment: Mexican Rodeo. It would seem that this pastime shouldn't differ fundamentally from its mate because of its close location and similarity of cultures. But Mexican rodeo has always stayed apart. Even equestrian sport, that has limitless tolerance towards horse tortures pushed out this Mexican pastime.

In the USA legislation against this entertainment is marginal, often compromised from cultural pressure to uphold Mexican heritage, so local journalists still hurl scandalous articles at the Latin Americans. This fact only makes us look closer and examine this phenomenon.

A short trip through history

Charreada (Mexican rodeo) came from Spain in the 18th century. On the American continent this entertainment appeared approximately in 1520, when Spanish conquistadors invaded the territory of modern Mexico.

At the beginning of the 18th century that particular "equestrian" pasttime settled down in local ranchos where men caught horses with lassoes to show courage and complete mastery as a charro (Mexican cowboy). In the USA beginning the the 1950's and continuing through the 60's upwards of 84 Charreada Associations formed, organizing events on a massive scale.

For the most part the events took place in the west and in the southwest (states of Arizona, California, Colorado, Texas, etc.). Nowadays all competitions are held under the auspices of these continuing or descendent associations.

The main point of the pastime

Charreada includes nine disciplines, three of which require a charro to throw a lasso on the fore limbs or hind limbs of a "wild" horse. After this manipulation the lassoed horse overbalances and falls on the ground at full tilt. For each "successful" fall the charro gains points. Later on, according to the amount of points scored, the winner is determined. As I have already mentioned, there are three types of roping:

- Piales en la lienzo — the rider ropes the hind limbs of a galloping horse bringing it to the ground;

- Manganas a pie — an unmounted cowboy ropes a galloping horse on the fore legs tripping it to the ground;

- Manganas a caballo — this is similar to manganas a pie except that the charro is mounted.

The romantic idea, on which the Mexican rodeo is based, is to show a fearless image of a man who skillfully tames an infuriated and raging horse. With a sinking heart the audience follows the young (or not so young) man who, in spite of the danger, pursues an unbroken, strong, free and unconquerable horse. Having caught and tamed the "wild" being the man becomes the hero.

It's quite an attractive legend… But we have to destroy it (we ask those amateurs of such Wild West romances to close this book so you can avoid pain during the breaking of your own stereotypes).

Let's start with the main victim of rodeo — the horse. Exhausted and in fact unwanted horses, which were bought for low prices at auctions, perform as wild and raging. So called "third parties" buy unwanted horses and lease them on weekends to participate in Mexican rodeo. To use that wild mustang our romantic hero (that courageous charro) pays $65.00 per day. Charros prefer smaller horses with Arabian roots because it's easier to knock them down.

When all the preparations for the rodeo are over (i. e. the audience has swallowed enough fire water to begin to shuffle and fuss, and all the charros have combed their moustaches and clapped on their enormous hats) the real fun begins.

The ring is a typical American rodeo ring, though in the Mexican province it can look quite simple without any excess, looking more like an unfortunate construction encircled with an ill-knocked-up wooden fence. A "wild" horse is allowed into the ring. A fleeting stroke by an electric prod creates an image of a raging mustang (small electric shockers can even be put into a palm).

During this foolish chase, the horse (remember she is an unwanted throwaway low value invalid) is roped and harshly tripped to the ground instantly obtaining countless musculoskeletal and neurological traumas. The most common traumas are limb fractures, broken necks, joint displacement, deep lacerated wounds (of heads, necks, limbs etc.), broken teeth, and, of course, rope burns.

There have been incidents known when horses in agony ran away and jumped over fences to escape from the torture. Of course they were caught and brought back as the audience whistled and hooted. But even respectful spectators suffer splinters from filthy fences being beaten into toothpicks.

Cathleen Doyle of the California Equine Council in her 1998 study visited 10 Mexican rodeos and examined 78 horses which were leased for those events. She found out that only two (!) horses remained alive after the five to six month season. Having received severe traumas the other horses died in the ring or in slaughterhouses. These statistics show perfectly the savagery and criminality of Mexican rodeo.

Legality

As it was pointed out at the beginning charreada is thrown out to the outskirts by equestrian sport. By saying "outskirts" we mean that in the USA this event is organized privately by small groups of people in back yard ranchos. For organizing charreada coordinators are imposed a fine at the rate of $1000 or imprisoned for six months (for organizing major charreado).

With the activity of animal rights groups, who cooperate with the mass media, and the consequent public opinion pressures on the states authorities allow them to pursue a policy of liquidation of the pastime. The number of states that admit to Mexican rodeo as being illegal is growing steadily.

As strange as it may seem there are charreada supporters and protectors who try to lobby for adoption of a law. Of course Mexicans are the loudest screamers and devoted supporters. One of the arguments is that they don't kill horses but only knock them down (on average one attempt in 10 is successful). They say the charreada is an irreplaceable part of original Mexican culture and the USA encroaches on the centuries-old Mexican traditions.

The Rodeo Cowboys Association defends this pastime, members of which realize the fatal consequences of a humane mood of American public opinion. They have seen a frightening example how what brought them crowds and good profit yesterday, today dies and repels. It's obvious for them that if rodeo becomes illegal it'll immediately stop the flow of funds (which supply their business) and will make the "classic" American rodeo dusty on the same shelf as Mexican rodeo as a reminder of human blindness and deafness to the horse's pain.

Georgi Gavrilenko,
Liza Kilina,
Nevzorov Haute Ecole students

APPENDIX 1

ENDOGENOUS MECHANISMS OF MODIFICATION OF PAIN SENSITIVITY IN HORSES

Anastasia Nekrasova,

Research Officer, Department of Genetics and Breeding,
Saint Petersburg University, Russia,
Nevzorov Haute École Research Centre Specialist

INTRODUCTION

There is quite a lot known nowadays about pain, anatomical structures and physiological processes which condition the processes of pain reception, perception, modification of this perception, emotional reactions to pain and the generation of response to pain. This article deals with two small but important aspects of pain sensation which are crucial for understanding how horses perceive pain and react to it. These aspects are responses to noxious stimuli and endogenous mechanisms of modification of pain sensitivity in horses.

1. RESPONSIVENESS TO NOXIOUS STIMULI

Despite numerous studies, science struggles to find a big difference in the pain perception of different species of large mammals. This is not surprising, as the biological purpose of pain is to warn an animal and to insure against factors which can cause harm to it. Subsequently, the reduction of the nociceptive system, the reduction of the ability to feel pain is unprofitable biologically speaking.

What does differ between species is the reponsiveness to noxious stimuli, i. e. the degree of the expression of the sense of pain and the amount of response to it. The responsiveness to noxious stimuli is defined considerably by inheritable reactions which are developed evolutionarily. It can also be modified depending on the individual's anatomic and physiological characteristics or as the consequence of acquired experience.

For example, primates, if harmed, cry loudly to get the attention of their "tribe members", they make faces and try to avoid making faces, try to avoid the harmful factor in any possible way or act defensively. Pigs show similar behavior. But most ungulates act completely differently. Most of them attempt to keep silent even if they are seriously wounded and try not to show any signs of injury, including... not tailing off their kin retreating from a carnivore. This is a display of an evolutionary adaptation. While crying, an ape or monkey attracts the attention of its family and they try to fend off the aggressor together. On the other hand, the defensive reaction of a herd of ungulates is built on the "don't stand out" principle: when a group of ungulates flees from a carnivore, it is hard for a carnivore to find its potential victim if all the animals are alike. The moment a carnivore takes to consider can save the lives of all the members of the herd. But if someone shows signs of weakness it becomes the target and, very possibly, the victim.

A lot of humans believe that other species display the degree of pain with loud cries like humans themselves do. So they consider vocalization to be the main indication of someone being in pain. But the vocalization of pain is defined by the inherited specific responsiveness. For example, pigs, if castrated without anesthesia, cry extremely loudly. But horses, on the other hand, stay silent during the same manipulation. They have much lower responsiveness to noxious stimuli, but feel the same pain. They stay silent while twitched, while their lips are torn with bits, while their legs break, while their hooves are pierced with nails, while suffering from laminitis, while being branded with cold or hot branding-irons. The last example gives stud-farm owners the cause to believe, basing on their "personal experience", that hot branding is almost painless for horses. This is not true.

The fact that a lot of people don't know anything on the matter of the responsiveness to noxious stimuli allows yahoos to cultivate the myth that horses, unlike humans, feel less pain; that the use of traumatic tools is painless for horses. According to the scientific studies, it is a myth.

2. ENDOGENOUS MECHANISMS OF MODIFICATION OF PAIN SENSITIVITY

The main characteristics of the nociceptive system is the threshold of its irritation (the pain threshold), i. e. its ability to activate only as the reaction towards harmful or nearly harmful stimulus.

Pain thresholds can differ in different representatives of one species. It depends on inherited anatomic and physiological characteristics such as the speed of the conduction of nervous impulses, the sensitivity of different receptors, the activity of mediator production, etc. For example, according to research, red-haired people need 20 percent more anesthesia than others. Scientists believe that the mutation which leads to changes in the pigment genesis of hair and skin also affects the mechanisms of pain sensitivity.

A pain threshold can differ in one organism depending on its state. There are situations when pain sensitivity can be higher or lower.

2.1. Hyperalgesia

Hyperalgesia is the state of enhanced pain sensitivity. In this state pain is felt spontaneously, without injury or irritation. It is divided into primary and secondary hyperalgesia. The former is found in injured tissues, the latter is located outside of the injured area.

During primary hyperalgesia the sensitivity of the pain receptor to the injuring stimuli is higher than normal in the injured areas. This is because in the injured area the inflammatory mediators are produced, such as bradykinin, prostaglandin and leukotriene, biogenous amines (histamine, acetylcholine, noradrenaline) as well as some other substances. While interacting with the corresponding receptors of the pain cells, these substances lower their threshold of excitation and make them more sensitive towards the mechanical and thermic stimuli. Thus primary hyperalgesia can be removed with local anesthesia.

During secondary hyperalgesia, an enhancing of the pain sensitivity can be seen at some distance from the injured area, for example, on the opposite side of the body. It is considered to be a consequence of the constant hyper-excitation of the nociceptive neurons of the spinothalamic tract, which is affected by the electrical excitation of the nociceptors of the injured area. The significant role of this mechanism is played by the P-substance which is produced by the neurons of the spinal chord. This P-substance enhances the signal ten-fold. The other significant substance here is serotonin, which enhances the overall excitation of the neurons. If hyper-excitation occurs, the neurons of the spinothalamic tract become sensitive to the mechanical irritation of their receptive field in the area of the secondary hyperalgesia. So, if local anesthetics are applied to the injured area, the secondary hyperalgesia won't reduce. But it can be treated with a chemical block of the neuron activity of the spinal dorsal horn.

The biological purpose of hyperalgesia is the pain sensitivity in the injured area being enhanced so the injured animal would treat this area more carefully and not allow even small irritation which can't damage the healthy tissues but are dangerous for the injured ones. So there is nothing peculiar about horses reacting violently even if the injured area is touched gently. It is important to keep in mind that pain-relief medication is not always necessary and sometimes can be even harmful because the horse would not treat his wound carefully enough.

A number of cortical structures are considered to be the part of the limbic system (rhinencephalon, piriform lobe, hyppocampus, callosal gyrus, amygdala), with subcortical structures (amygdaloid complex, interseptum), structures of the mesencephalon and the diencephalon (thalamic and hypothalamic nuclei). The limbic system closely interacts with the cortex. It is considered that the limbic system

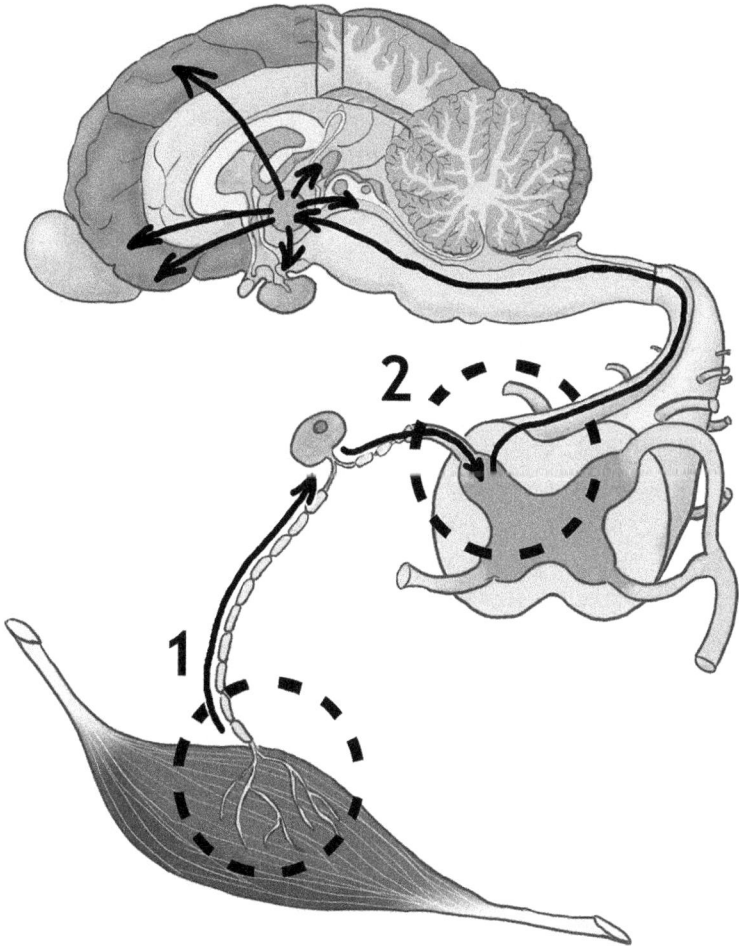

© Anastasia Nekrasova

Arrows mark the passage of a signal from a pain receptor to different
structures of the brain. See explanations in the text:
1 – Primary; 2 – Secondary

takes part in the regulation of vegetative functions, organization of a number of behavioral acts (sexual, defensive, feeding), forming of motivation and emotion, the process of memory preservation and regulation of sleep. But some studies question the theory that the limbic system takes part in the forming of the sense of pain.

The thing they call in equestrian sport "bit chewing" is a result of hyperalgesia. The horse tries to move the bit from the injured and thus more sensitive areas to the less injured and less painful ones.

A state of hyperalgesia can be caused by influence of the cerebral cortex. When pain is anticipated consciously and is feared by a person, a hyper-excitation of the nociceptive neurons occurs and as a result, any painful effect is perceived as a more painful one.

2.2. Endogenous hypo- and analgesia

Besides the mechanisms of enhanced pain sensitivity there are no less necessary mechanisms of the reducing of the pain sensitivity in the horse's organism. The reduction of pain sensitivity is called hypoalgesia. The absence of pain sensitivity is called analgesia.

These states are caused by the endogenous (produced by the organism itself) opioid substances — endorphin and enkephalin. Under their influence the nociceptive tracts remain activated but the expansion of the pain impulse is blocked in the junctions of the neurons. Pain is suppressed in the junctions of the neurons in the spinal chord, the gray matter of the Sylvian aqueduct, thalamus, hypothalamus or the limbic system.

Besides the inner opiates there are other substances which are connected with the sense of pain in animals: neurotensin, angiotensin, oxytocin, serotonin and some others. Some of them can reduce the pain 1000 times more effectively than endorphin and enkephalin.

Neurosecretive structures (Sylvian aqueduct, etc.) are affected by the cerebral cortex. That is why the pain sensitivity depends on the emotional and motivational state of an animal: fear, rage, joy and motivations of hunger, thirst, etc.

The powerful afferent flow from the other receptive neurons (tactile, acoustical, etc.) can reduce the primary pain sensitivity with the help of the "switching" of the interneurons for the reception of the more powerful signal. This way the nervous system chooses the most powerful irritation as its priority. And this is how new or more acute pain can cause the reduction of the sensitivity to the weaker pain. A horse would treat more carefully the area which is in more pain.

During equestrian competitions you can see horses stop obeying their riders as they feel increasing pain in their mouths, backs, necks and legs. But riders can quickly regain control by causing more acute pain.

2.3. Emotion, motivation and other causes of analgesia

In the healthy organism the sense of pain forms only two emotions: fear and aggression. They cause one or the other form of defensive behavior. Control over the horse in equestrian sports is based on the infliction of pain or the threat of causing of pain thus forming the subduing emotion of fear. Any aggression is suppressed.

The biological purpose of fear is to enhance the individual's perception of possible (but not always obvious) danger and to take immediate action to avoid contact with the hazard. Depending upon the irritant, circumstances, personal characteristics, previous experience and present state of a horse, the consequences of fear can be the attempts to hide, flee or fight. A horror can trigger the mechanisms of hypoalgesia and even analgesia through the endorphin-opioid system described above. In the wild this ability is essential for a horse to run away from a predator without displaying injuries and to have a chance to save his life, for example. In equestrian sport this pain-relieving mechanism explains the rebellion and the bolting of horses. For example, sometimes a rider cannot stop a horse even with a very powerful impact of the bit or the whip, i.e. a massive pain-infliction. The degree of the pain impact which can make it possible for a rider to stop a horse in such a situation depends on the degree of the analgesia of the horse's organism. If the analgesia is total no pain can stop a horse. But the pain impact can, on the contrary, enhance the emotion of fear and its escalation into aggression or fury.

Aggression also can trigger the mechanism of the anesthetization. Biologically it is necessary for a horse while fighting with another horse, for example. During a fight it is more important to overcome the opponent here and now and later take care of the wounds. In equestrian sport the rebellion of a horse often occurs under the effect of defensive aggression with accompanying hypoalgesia which helps a horse to fight the pain. But, as with fear, the acute pain which is more powerful than the degree of hypoalgesia can make it possible for the rider to take control over the horse or vice versa — enhance the aggression.

Strong aggression escalates to become fury. While furious, a horse is in total analgesia and stops feeling pain. That is why during stallion fights horses can pay no attention to very serious wounds. And these are the moments when the most dreadful unstoppable rebellions occur for the parasaite-human. All the common methods of control — via pain — don't work anymore. A horse begins to feel pain only after he calms down.

The escalation of fear into the aggression or even fury is connected with the fact that the centers of these emotions in the brain are situated not only in the amygdula, but also in special nuclei of the posterior hypothalamus which are placed very closely to each other. The powerful irritation which causes the excitation of the centers of fear in the hypothalamus can spread and cause the excitation of the centers of aggression (fury). That is why the emotion of fear can relatively easily transform into aggression and fury.

Biologically this ability can help the organism, when the usual response caused by fear (the attempts to elude the hazard) are ineffective. In such circumstances the brian activates another program, defensive aggression or even fury which can help the organism to survive. In a frightened animal which can not run away the fear will transform into fury and it will fight desperately, often causing its opponent to retreat. Even a small rat can be dangerous in this state for large aggressor like dog or human. This biological fact has fostered the proverb: "Dangerous like a beast driven into a corner".

Positive emotion of joy can also provoke hypoalgesia. It is known that horses with lameness and other illnesses if let into the paddock will burden their injured legs while playing. The hypoalgesia happens with the help of the endorphins.

Emotions of pain, thirst and sexual desire can also cause hypoalgesia. As a consequence, more active resistance towards painful factors occurs. A horse can ignore his own injuries or the pain inflicted by a human. It is a common fact that the horses harnessed in some noble's or even king's carriage often had driven the carriage into the river to drink some water despite the cruel bits used for carriage horses. Often horses fight bits to get to the green grass. And every horse-user knows how it is difficult or even impossible to control a stallion who has scented a mare (or even more dangerous, a mare in heat) nearby. This is even incorporated in safety arrangements.

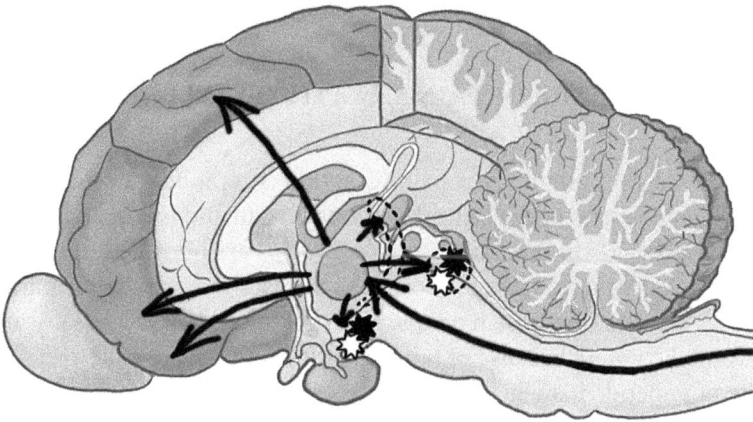

© Anastasia Nekrasova

The centers of fear and aggression are marked.
The amygdala won't be seen on the sagital projection,
so here only the projection of its placement is marked)

During chronic pain self-hypoalgesia occurs. Acute pain can put an animal into a comatose condition. A dying animal often self-narcotizes and at this stage the applying of pain-killers is ineffective.

As was mentioned above, because the neuro-secreting structures are influenced by cerebral cortex, pain sensitivity depends on the "mood". It is known, that people who had been warned of the pain beforehand can prepare themselves for the pain and bear it more easily. A horse can not tell us directly how he feels, but often a horse, who is treated by the human he knows and trusts, reacts more calmly and, likely, feels less pain.

3. INBORN ABSENCE OF PAIN SENSITIVITY OR ENHANCED PAIN SENSITIVITY

As we can see, the system of the pain reception is complicated, closely related with other structures of the central nervous system and is crucial for the survival of the organism. But sometimes organisms are born without pain sensitivity. I haven't found any mention of such cases in horses, and in humans only a few are described. Such people often get injured, have a lot of scars and burns and die young because of traumas or infections. For example, they often die of appendicitis which they hadn't felt. Scientists discovered that this pathology is connected with a mutation of the gene SCN9A which encodes the protein which takes part in the transportation of the sodium ions through the membranes of the neurons of the pain receptors.

On the other hand, there are people who feel acute pain even if the impact is weak — such as a mere scratch. This can also be an inborn mutation.

It is clear, that an animal with such pathology, even a domestic one, would not live for long. A horse with an inborn hyperalgesia would be useless for exploitation because he would overreact towards the usual methods of control. And if a horse would not feel any pain, humans would not be able to control him as well. The higher the degree of the hypoalgesia, the more power a human has to use on the subduing instruments, this way causing more injuries to overcome the high threshold of pain sensitivity. In total analgesia a horse can not be controlled at all.

Either a horse feels pain in the current moment, or not, all the traumas will stay traumas and the pain will come later. That is why, however humans may think of it, any kind of force control of a horse is the causation of injuries to an intelligent creature in order to subdue it.

APPENDIX 2

THE FORCE OF COMMON AND JERK TORQUE IMPACT OF CONTROL MEANS USED IN EQUESTRIAN SPORTS (SNAFFLE, CURB)

ПРАВИТЕЛЬСТВО САНКТ-ПЕТЕРБУРГА
КОМИТЕТ ПО ЗДРАВООХРАНЕНИЮ
**САНКТ-ПЕТЕРБУРГСКОЕ
ГОСУДАРСТВЕННОЕ УЧРЕЖДЕНИЕ
ЗДРАВООХРАНЕНИЯ
«БЮРО СУДЕБНО-МЕДИЦИНСКОЙ
ЭКСПЕРТИЗЫ»**
195067, Санкт-Петербург,
Екатерининский пр., 10
тел. (7-812) 544-1717;факс (7-812) 545-0340
ОКПО 01932390 ОКОГУ 07185
E-mail: sudmed@zdrav.spb.ru

14.12.2006 г. № 356 /01-4

А К Т

испытаний по установлению силы
рывкового и штатного воздействий средств управления,
используемых в конном спорте (мундштук, трензель),
на рот лошади

Цель испытаний: установление максимальной силы рывкового и штатного воздействий средств управления, используемых в конном спорте (мундштук, трензель), на рот лошади.

Задачи испытаний:
– установление силы рывкового усилия средств управления, используемых в конном спорте (мундштук, трензель), на рот лошади при воздействии людей, обладающих разной физической силой;
– установление силы штатного усилия (относительно медленного натяжения) средств управления, используемых в конном спорте (мундштук, трензель), на рот лошади при воздействии людей, обладающих разной физической силой.

Условия постановки экспериментов:
Экспертные исследования проводились на манекенах (синтетических моделях), геометрические и механические показатели которых полностью соответствовали голове лошади (с полуоткрытым ртом) в момент воздействия на нее средств управления.
Перед экспериментами манекены (синтетические модели) головы лошади прочно закрепляли в положении, обеспечивающем обычное соотношение рук «наездника», повода и головы лошади в момент воздействия на нее средств управления.
В качестве средств управления ходе экспертизы были применены стандартные средства управления в виде мундштука и трензеля, выполненные из желтого металла.
Для укрепления на голове средств управления (мундштука и трензеля) были использованы штатная система ремней в виде «уздечки» или «оголовья».
В экспериментах рычаг, придающий воздействию силу и эффективность, т.н. «повод» был идентичен применяемому в конном спорте.
Воздействие осуществлялось через прочный повод (с длиной стороны 1 м).

NEVZOROV HAUTE ÉCOLE
RESEARCH CENTRE

GOVERNMENT OF SAINT-PETERSBURG
HEALTH PROTECTION COMMITTEE
STATE INSTITUTE
OF HEALTH PROTECTION
OF SAINT-PETERSBURG
"COURT-MEDICAL EXPERTIZING BUREAU"
195067, Saint-Petersburg,
Ekaterininskiy pr. 10
tel. (7-812) 544-1717, fax. (7-812) 545 0340
OKPO 01932390 OKOGU 07185
E-mail: sudmed@zdray.spb.ru
14.12.2006 No 356 /01-4

STATEMENT

of examinations to define the force
of common and jerk torque impact of control means
used in equestrian sports (snaffle, curb)
upon a horse's mouth

Purpose of examinations: definition of the maximum force of jerk torque and common impact of control means used in equestrian sports (snaffle, curb) upon a horse's mouth.

Examinational tasks:

– definition of the maximum force of jerk torque impact of control means used in equestrian sports (snaffle, curb) upon a horse's mouth by people possessing different physical strength.
– definition of the maximum force of common impact of control means used in equestrian sports (snaffle, curb) upon a horse's mouth by people possessing different physical strength.

Experimental conditions:

Experiments were carried out on mannequins (synthetic models), with geometric and mechanical properties that are completely corresponding to head of a horse (with mouth half-opened) at the moment of impact of equipment for control.

Before the beginning of every experiment mannequins (synthetic models) of a horse head were firmly fixed in a position, providing a common physical correlation between rider's hands, reins and the head of a horse as ridden in the moment of impact of control means.

As control means standard control means in the forms of a snaffle and a curb, made of metal of yellow color were used.

For proper fixation of control means (snaffle and curb) on the mannequin head a common strap system (in the form of a "bridle" and a "head-band") was used.

In the experiments performed, the lever, providing correspondent force and efficiency (so called "reins"), was identical to the one used in equestrian sports.

Impact was exercised through durable reins (with a long side of 1m in length).

For determination of the square of mechanical contact impact upon a horse's mouth a special device was used, commonly utilized in medico-criminalist expertise.

The total impact force was measured by a special dynamometer with a pointer fixated at maximum value and a scale up to 350 kg with scaling factor equal to 5 kg.

During the experiments the following people were selected to be producers of physical effects (jerk and common drawing), entailing painful impact on the horse's mouth:

- a boy of 13 years old
- young woman of 23 years old
- a man of 43 years old

Examinational results:

In the course of experiments carried out it had been defined, that:

1. The total maximum impact force of reins upon the horse head mannequin was fixated at the respective levels:
- for drawing: from 50 to 100 kg;
- for jerking: from 220 to 300 kg.

2. The impact force of the subject metal instruments (control means) named "a snaffle" and "a curb" aggregates (per 1 sq. cm. of mouth surface):
- for drawing: from 50 to 100 kg;
- for an average force jerk: from 180 to 220 kg;
- for a strong jerk: over 300 kg.

3. Mechanical impacts of mentioned intensity, registered during experiments, may lead to various damage of oral cavity tissues: from abrasions, hemorrhages, mucous tunic ruptures up to compound wounds and even to bones being broken.

Besides that, detected levels of maximum impact force upon the horse head mannequin, especially for strong jerks, may be dangerous in the way of causing damage to ligament-articularis apparatus of the cervical part of a vertebral column of a horse.

Medico-legal experts:

Deputy Chief of Bureau for Expertise
Doctor of Medical Science, Professor
Honored Inventor of Russian Federation
V. D. Isakov

Head of Corpse Expertise Department
Candidate of Medical Science
Doctor of Higher Qualification Category
V. E. Sysoev

Head of Nevzorov Haute École Research Centre
A. G. Nevzorov

APPENDIX 3

"PUNISHMENT" IMPACT ON A HORSE'S MOUTH BY THE "SNAFFLE BIT" USED IN EQUESTRIAN SPORTS

Independent Laboratory Experiment.

Investigation of the amount of force which riders apply to the horse's mouth with a bit for typical riding and purposes of punishment.

By Lydia Nevzorova

Abridged version

The purpose of this study was to consider methods that allow an objective assessment of the welfare of horses undergoing training. It was demonstrated that high levels of force are applied to the horse's mouth for punishment via reins and bit, which causes pain, serious injuries and can be considered cruelty.

ACKNOWLEDGEMENTS

This study would not have been possible without the assistance of forensics experts of the State Institute of Health Protection of St. Petersburg: Deputy Chief of "Forensics Bureau" for Expertise, Doctor of Medical Science, Professor, and Honored Inventor of Russian Federation V.D. Isakov and Head of Corpse Expertise Department Candidate of Medical Science Doctor of Higher Qualification Category V. E. Sysoev.

ABSTRACT

There are reports available regarding the use of the bit in typical circumstances. However, no evidence of the amount of force applied to the horse's mouth in equine sport in the case of punishment was available. The purpose of this project is to acquire that evidence.

The report describes a laboratory experiment with several selected training techniques that are used in this modern age. The amount of pressure that was actually applied by six riders of different qualifications to the mouth of the horse by pulling the reins was determined with a dynamometer attached to each rein. The experiment tested "riding in collection", "halt" and two forms of "punishment" forces applied by the rider. *The mean rein tension for work was 65 N, for halt 137 N; for punishment method #1 1002 N and 1240.5 N for punishment method #2. (N = Newtons).* The maximum impact force of the reins upon the horse head mannequin was recorded at the level of 1754 N. Mechanical impacts of the intensities registered during experiments might lead to various damages to oral cavity tissues. The author is of the opinion that bit punishment represents pain and cruelty. After the experiment, all participants were interviewed. Common methods of bit punishment, the amount of rein tension, and why they were applied to the horse's mouth were discussed and analysed. The work concludes with suggestions for future research.

1. INTRODUCTION

Attention was called to the fact that training methods used across equestrian disciplines could jeopardize equine welfare. While it was proven that the bit is the cause of many diseases, disorders, and injuries (Cook, 2003), it is still used in equitation. The term 'cruelty' is still not attributed to physical punishment, harm, pain or injury that may happen in equine sport.

Some studies were conducted to determine the appropriate rein contact required for specific movements, in particular the lower range of tensions (Warren-Smith et al., 2007). Riders are encouraged to maintain the lightest contact using just the weight of the reins (Wynmalen, 1985). In practice, this is rarely accomplished (Ödberg and Bouissou, 1999; McGreevy et al., 2005; Cook, 2007). At the same time, no studies were presented in regard to the higher ranges of rein tension and maximum tension. The most detrimental methods used for punishment tend to be avoided in discussions.

It is impossible to discuss appropriate use of reinforcements while avoiding misconceptions if it has not been clarified which methods of punishment riders commonly use. Therefore, it was decided to carry out an experiment that defines the force used by riders of different experiences and qualifications in punishment with the bit. The aim in this report was to use actual methods that allow an objective assessment of the welfare of horses undergoing training, and bring forth an overall awareness. The experiment was conducted on a mannequin, as the author considered the procedure to be too cruel to test on live horses.

1.1. Issue of Bit Punishment and Cruelty in Equine sport — Previous Studies Review

While there have not been in-depth studies regarding the forces that are applied to a horse's mouth via the reins and bit during punishment, there are some studies that focus on 'normal' rein tension using tensiometry.

Bit induced behaviour problems, diseases and injuries were studied in depth mainly in numerous works of Cook. Cook was the first to raise attention to cruelty, which is defined as the infliction of unnecessary (avoidable) pain or distress (Cook, 2002). Aside from Cook, only Nevzorov (2004) attributed the term "cruelty" to bit-induced problems and specific methods used in equine sport. Cook (2003) declared that the use of a bit in an area as sensitive as the oral cavity would cause pain to the horse, whether or not the rider or handler is aware of its infliction. The bit conflicts with the myological and physiological nature of a horse (Cook, 2003). He also reported that the bit is a cause of over a hundred behavioural problems, and more than 40 different diseases (Cook, 2008).

Pain frightens a horse (Cook 2007a), causing physical damage (Ödberg and Bouissou, 1999). It creates soreness, injuries such as mandibular periostitis (Clayton, 2004; Bennett, 2006) and bone spurs in the diastema (Edwards, 2000; Cook, 2002; Tell et al.,2008), dorsal displacement of the soft palate and facial neuralgia (Cook 2007; Warren-Smith, et al., 2007). Rollin (2000) and Bennett (2009) reported that tongue lacerations are the most obvious injuries associated with the improper use of bits as well as injuries to the bars and other tissues. Johnson (2003) suggested that "horses and riders can greatly benefit from the comfort enabled by surgical removal of mandibular periostitis" and that "the horse will gradually forget about the previous pain". However Johnson did not explain how he obtained the evidence that the horse forgets the pain. He reported that most horses with damage to the mandibular bone are performance horses ridden with bit contact (Johnson, 2003).

In addition, the bit triggers inappropriate digestive system reflexes that are incompatible with the physiology of exercise (Cook, 2007). Use of the bit results in obstruction of the nasopharyngeal and laryngeal airway (Cook, 2003) and erosion of the first three cheek teeth on both sides of the jaw as a result of the bit being pulled backwards over the crowns of the teeth (Cook, 2009).

Behavioral problems account for up to 66 percent of euthanasia in young horses (Ödberg and Bouissou, 1999). Evidence of pain can be a root cause of undesired behavioral responses when riding horses (McLean et al. 2005). One such example of pain resulting from a horse being unable to free itself from the pressure of a bit due to overly tight reins is an occurrence called 'bridle lameness' (McLean et. al., 2005). Failure to escape pressure produced by excessive rein tension could result in a state of learned helplessness (pain tolerance in animals exposed to repeated and/or unavoidable aversive stimuli) as well as anhedonia and increased health problems such as gastric ulcers (Hall et al., 2008). According to Laskov (2007), consequences of the blow produced by a bit can be defined as traumatic shock in horses (Laskov, 1997). However, he agreed with the use of pain for "achieving better results". He explained his point: "Strong pain can be applied but only in the case of developing or perfecting conditional reflexes of a horse" (Laskov, 1997).

Frustrated trainers often try bits of greater severity (Rollin, 2000; McGreevy, 2009). The severity of a bit depends on the points of pressure, the diameter and texture of the mouthpiece (Wyse et al., 2000). The textures such as twisted wire, rollers, slow twists and chains greatly increase the pressure and severity exerted by the horseman (Wyse et al., 2000). All types of bits can press the lips and cheeks against points or premolar caps on the upper cheek teeth (Bennett, 2001; Clayton, 2007).

Rollin (2000) reported that the current agenda in equitation science focuses on the development of "correction" instrumentation, such as saw-chain bits, which are readily available to riders who are having problems getting horses to respond to milder bits.

Numerous horses seem to live in a constant state of stress being unable to avoid punishment (Ödberg, 1987). Hall et al. (2008) concluded that there are many aversive techniques used in horse training that compromise the horse's welfare, both physically and psychologically.

A recent study indicates growing evidence that there is a gap in the knowledge of professional equestrian coaches (Warren-Smith & McGreevy, 2008). According to McLean (2004), instead of actually solving the problem by analyzing the causes and readjusting the training, trainers often advocate to increase pressure, to use whips, spurs and stronger bits.

Surprisingly, aside from few researchers such as Friedberger, Cook, and Hall who speak openly about the pain and cruelty of the bit, others do not use the term "cruelty" and do not attribute cruelty to methods used in equine sport. They discussed positive and negative reinforcement using terms such as "pressure", "tension", "conflict behavior" and advise riders to use as light aids as possible (Warren et al., 2002; McGreevy, 2004). Wynmalen, (1985) declared that one of the goals of classical equitation is to ride using almost imperceptible stimuli applied to the mouth. Warren et al. (2002) claim that any effective horse training should be based on clear and consistent signals from the trainer as well as a proper understanding of the horse's behavior and learning capacities. According to McGreevy (2004), "the aim of training is to install signals (cues) that result in predictable behaviour patterns".

However, in the same study he reported that a mismatch between horse and rider could sometimes appear as jerks or struggles between the two parties (McGreevy, 2004). McGreevy (2009) stated that punishment is often incorrectly used while training horses, and may in fact lead to further behavioral problems, instead of suppressing existing ones. The main reason is that punishment is non-directed, meaning that it has the potential to suppress a behavior, but will not enhance an alternative one (McGreevy, 2009).

Almost all studies mentioned that reinforcement often was applied inappropriately and that abusive, irrelevant or redundant bit pressures jeopardize horse welfare (Miller, 1995; Warren et al., 2002; McLean, 2003; Mc-Greevy, 2004; Heleski, 2009). McGreevy (2009) identified a continuum between poorly timed negative reinforcement and punishment. It explores some of the problems of non-contingent punishment and the prospect of learned helplessness and experimental neurosis. McGreevy (2009) suggested that techniques such as punishment should only be used as a last resort, and even then, with the utmost care. He concluded by introducing the concept of ethical equitation. Chamove et al. (2002) categorized the tension in reins subjectively as being "tense", "intermediate" or "relaxed or loose". It was found that nothing was said about jerking actions for punishment. However, Clayton et al. (2003) highlighted the need for objective measurements of rein tensions applied to horses and concluded that the strain gage transducer system was valid for it.

1.2. Hypothesis

The present study tested the null hypothesis that if a horse is punished for "inappropriate" behavior while being ridden in a snaffle bit there will be no serious change in rein tension and thus force applied to the horse's mouth. The alternative hypothesis was that there would be significant change and that rein tension would rise dramatically to a level that is enough to cause serious pain and injury.

1.3. Conclusion

Previous studies clearly demonstrate that the FEI, equine and veterinary sciences were well aware of the pain caused by using a bit by at least 1970, when Friedberger (1970) reported that misuse of the bit can cause pain and injury. However, equine science finds it acceptable to use the bit as a painful control aid and allows its application up to now.

Although all authors urge that using the bit incorrectly may jeopardize the horse's welfare (Warren, 2002; McGreevy, 2004; Clayton, 2005; Bennett, 2006), further scientific research into equine behavior and learning is needed to create accurate parameters to measure welfare.

Recent studies have developed a technique to accurately measure rein tension (Warren-Smith et al., 2006), which should give riders the ability to minimize pressure on the horse's mouth by using a lighter contact, reducing discomfort from the bit (Hall et al., 2008). However measurement methods are not commonly used in real training.

1.4. Objectives

Measure rein tension for working in collection, halt, and two methods of bit punishment.

Interview participants and investigate their opinions in regard to the methods of rein tension they use.

2. METHODOLOGY

2.1. Introduction

The experiment was carried out at a State Institute of Health Protection of St. Petersburg "Forensics Bureau" in collaboration with forensics experts, who provide credibility for the project.

2.2. Details of Laboratory Equipment.

Experiments were carried out on mannequins (synthetic models) with geometric and mechanical properties that correspond to the head of a horse. It was possible to open the mouth of the mannequins part way at the moment of bit impact to simulate a real equine jaw.

To determine the force of impact upon a horse's mouth, we used a dynamometer with a pointer that remains fixed to record the maximum amount of force that had been applied and a scale which records up to 350 kilograms in increments of 0.5 kg. For these tests, dynamometer sensors were attached to both reins to measure the tensions on the left and right sides separately. The data was recorded and downloaded into a computer for further analyses, and presented in tables.

Before the beginning of every experiment, mannequins (synthetic models) of a horse's head were firmly fixed in position, providing the usual physical correlation between a rider's hands, reins and the head of a mounted horse at the moment of bit impact.

A standard bit, in the form of single-jointed snaffle bit, was used. The bits were made of stainless steel metal and weighed 250 g. For proper attachment of the bit on the mannequin's head, a common strap system (in the form of a "bridle" with a noseband) was used. In the experiments performed, the systems for transmitting force (commonly called "reins") were attached to the bit and were identical to those used in equestrian sports. The reins were made from leather (with a 1 m length, a 1.2 cm width and a 0.2 cm thickness).

2.3. Participants

During the experiments, three professional riders and three non-professional riders were randomly selected to produce the physical effects. The three professionals were as follows: a 13-year-old junior dressage rider (#1), a 25-year-old female international dressage rider and trainer (#2), and a 45-year-old male eventer and instructor (#3). The non-professional riders were: a 16-year old girl with a year of experience (#4), a 25-year old man with ten years of pleasure riding experience (#5), and a 40-year old woman with five years of amateur jumper experience (#6).

All participants were informed about the purpose of the experiment with the same phrase: "The common methods of bit use in riding will be tested in regards to the force applied to the horse's mouth." The participants were asked to behave as if they were riding a horse in the usual manner, and to demonstrate common methods of controlling the horse with a bit.

2.4. Details of Work Regime During Investigation.

Tension was measured and recorded after every rein pull, after every subsequent transfer of force to the bit on the mannequin.

All participants were asked to demonstrate four methods of rein use that s/he uses in his/her everyday practice.

Recorded data was then sorted to identify the maximum amount of force applied to the horse's mouth in different circumstances. These were categorized into: "riding in collection", "halt" and two methods of "punishment" in the case of "undesired behaviour of the horse" (the horse denying a request, rebelling to the aids).

The first and second methods of punishment tested have both external and internal differences. Method 1 represents a series of sharp, direct blows by the bit and the reins are jerked in sawing motion one after another at high speed (about two to four jerks from the elbow in one series). In the use of method 2, there is a very firm rein grip in one hand, which is typically pressed against the horse's neck, while the other hand executes a very strong pull backward. The rider's elbow goes back as far as possible, with the fixed hand creating the leverage.

Separate data was collected for left and right rein tensions and presented in tables.

When each rider finished the test, s/he answered questions on his/her opinion of the methods of bit use they demonstrated. The questions were about the control by the rider, the obedience of the horse, and how often they use the methods of punishment.

2.5. Conclusion

The experiment was carried out in the presence of witnesses. The events were independent, as the performance in the experiment is not affected by the performance of the preceding one. The strength of this finding provides sufficient evidence to warrant further investigation on a larger sample size, allowing serious statistical analysis.

3. RESULTS

The results refuted the null hypothesis and upheld the alternative hypothesis.

The experiment carried out demonstrated that the mean rein tension for work was 65 N, for halt 137 N; for punishment method #1 1002 N, and 1240.5 N for punishment method #2.

In the course of experiments carried out it was defined that the total maximum impact force of both reins upon the horse mannequin was measured at working tension from 3 to 10 kg; for halt: from 8 kg to 24 kg. For punishment

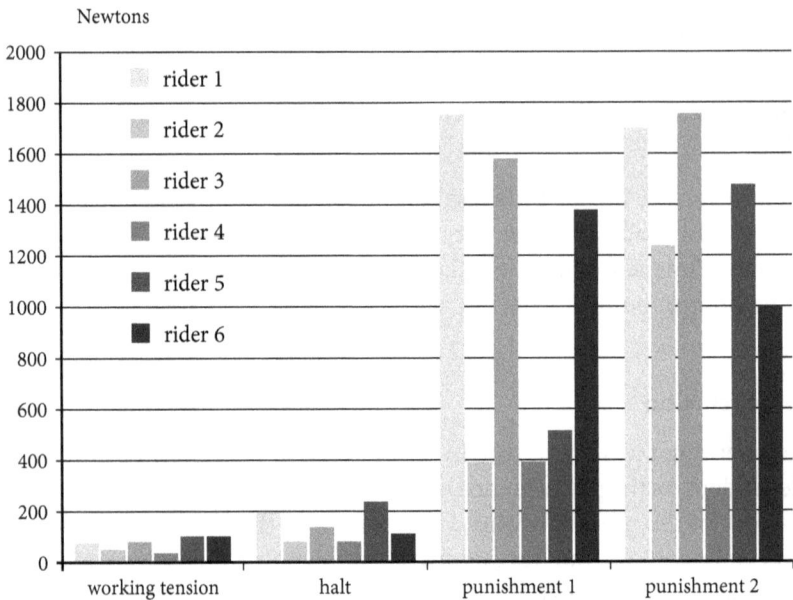

Maximum Rein Tension Registered in Experiment

**Results: Fig. 1 Rein tension applied to the horse's mouth
(data for right and left reins were combined).
The results are presented in Newtons.**

from method #1: from 40 kg to 179 kg and for punishment from method # 2 from 29 kg to 179 kg. The results are presented in Table 1.

In order to compare results with results of previous studies it was decided to calculate the combined rein tension of the right and left hand and present the data in Table 2 and Figure 1.

In the same table and for the same purposes the results of overall tension are presented in Newtons. The data obtained was multiplied by a coefficient of 9.8, as Clayton, (2005) and Warren et al. (2006) suggested that rein tension should be measured in Newtons because it is spread via the bit over the mouth surface.

After implementation of the experiment, all six participants answered the Questionnaire. The answers are presented in Table 3.

4. DISCUSSION

4.1. Introduction

Although in-depth statistical analysis was not possible in the experiment, the preliminary results offer very strong evidence that the results are not random.

Despite the fact that bitting has several negative aspects is it not an instrument for the rider to punish the horse (Bennett, 2006). Bennett (2006) declared that the well-trained rider is able to communicate with the horse primarily with the seat and leg aids. This was an idealistic approach, which did not correlate with study of Cook (2006); McGreevy (2007); Warren (2008), as well as with studies of Bennett himself.

The results of the present study are consistent with the findings of researchers such as Cook, that "to communicate painlessly, safely and effectively using a rod of steel in the horse's mouth is a skill that even a master horseman cannot achieve" (Cook, 2006).

4.2. Interpretation of Results

The tensions recorded for contact in the current trial were considerably stronger than those reported previously.

Rein Tension Data Obtained from Dynamometer in Kilograms

Rider #	Riding in collection/Working rein tension.		Halt: Both reins simultaneously drawn back with sub-maximal force		Punishment method #1: Fast jerk by reins from one side to the other (sawing motion)		Punishment method #2: One rein is fixed, while the other is jerked back with great force and speed from the elbow (pulley rein)	
Rein:	Right	Left	Right	Left	Right	Left	Right	Left
1	3.5	3.5	10	9.5	90.5	89	143.5	30
2	2.5	2.5	4	4	20	19.5	101	25
3	4	4	7	7	81.5	80	150.5	28.5
4	1.5	1.5	4	4	20	20	25	4
5	5	5	12	12	25.5	27	130	21
6	3.5	3.5	5.5	5.5	70.5	71	84	17

Results: Table 1. Table showing rein-tension for left and right reins by six riders demonstrating their usual methods of riding and punishment with plain reins and snaffle bit.

Overall Rein Tension in Kilograms and Newtons

Rider #	Riding in collection		Halt		Punishment #1		Punishment #2	
	KG	N	KG	N	KG	N	KG	N
1	7	68.6	19.5	191.1	179	1754.2	173.5	1700.3
2	5	49	8	78.4	39.5	387.1	126	1235.8
3	8	78.4	14	137.2	161.5	1582.7	179	1754.2
4	3	29.4	8	78.4	40	392	29	284.2
5	10	98	24	235.2	52.5	514.5	151	1479.8
6	7	68.6	11	107.8	141	1381.8	101	989.8

Results: Table 2. Rein tension applied to the horse's mouth (data for right and left reins were combined). The results presented in kilograms and Newtons

Questionnaire. Bit punishment in Equestrian Sport

Riders #	1	2	3	4	5	6
Is bit punishment painful for the horse?	Yes	No	Yes	No	No	Yes
How often do you apply the methods of punishment per day?	2-20	3-15	3-4	2-3	1	1-25
Are you aware of the methods you use?	No	No	No	No	No	No
Is there anything bad about inflicting pain on the horse?	no	no	no	yes	no	no
Is the pain caused by punishment possible for the horse to bear?	yes	yes	yes	yes	yes	yes
Where did you learn these methods?	From qualified trainer	In riding school	From FEI trainer	From instructor and stable staff	In riding school	From the stable mates
Is it possible to avoid punishment using the bit?	No	No	No/sometimes	No	No	No

Riders #	1	2	3	4	5	6
Do judges pay attention to the bit punishment methods in training and competition?	No	No	No	No	No	No
Have you ever been disqualified for the methods you used?	No	No	No	No	No	No
Are you amazed by the results of the test?	Yes	Yes	Yes	Yes	Yes	Yes
Do you know and apply other techniques of punishment with the bit?	Yes	Yes	Yes	Yes	Yes	Yes
Is it worth it to cause pain for the sake of Equine Sport?	Yes	Yes	Yes	Not sure	Yes	Yes
Are you going to change your methods of punishment after you find out the forces the bit applies to the horse's mouth?	No	No	No	I will think	No	No

Riders #	1	2	3	4	5	6
Do you feel stress, or fear during competition and training?	Yes	Yes	Yes	Yes	Yes	Yes
Does stress influence your riding style?	Yes	Yes	Yes	Yes	Yes	Yes
Do you punish more or less in public?	It depends on the horse's behaviour.	Milder	The same way	No difference	Milder	No difference
Do you consider it normal to inflict pain for bad behaviour?	Yes	Yes	Yes	Not sure	Yes	Yes
Have you ever become angry with yourself or the horse while training?	Yes	Yes	Yes	Yes	Yes	Yes
Are you afraid when the horse behaves 'badly'?	No	Sometimes	Yes	Yes	Yes	Sometimes
Do you feel more power for punishment when you are angry?	Yes	Yes	Yes	Yes	Yes	Yes

Riders #	1	2	3	4	5	6
Are you sure that you are always punishing the horse adequately for its behaviour?	Yes	No	Yes	No	Yes	No
Do you punish using the bit when you are angry or distressed for no particular reason?	Some-times	No	It may happen	No	Yes	It hap-pens
Do you have the moral right to punish the horse with pain?	Yes	Yes	Yes	Yes	Yes	Yes

Results: Table 3.

Interview with six equestrians who participated in the experiment.

As no previous research was processed for the use of punishment force, only the force applied for the "riding in collection" tension and "halt" could be compared with results of previous reports. Preuschoft et al. (1995) recorded between 50 and 75 N for a "normal" workout. In later work, Preuschoft et al. (1999) recorded tensions between approximately 6 and 75 N, similar to those of Clayton et al. (2003), who recorded rein tension in the range of 10–60 N, with 60 N for halt. It contrasted with results of de Cartier d'Yves and Ödberg (2005) who recorded up to 14 N and Warren-Smith et al. (2005) who reported 20 N and 9 N as a mean rein tension at a trot in a later report (Warren-Smith, 2006). Later, Warren-Smith et al. (2006) found that the overall mean tension needed in riding (including halt) was 7.4 ± 0.7 N, and that normal contact can be maintained at 3.9 N. In the current study, the mean for working tension was in the range of 29 – 98 N (65 N), and 78.4- 235 N (138 N) for the halt. The highest tension recorded in each gait by Clayton (2005) was 43 N at walk, 51 N at trot and 104 N in canter.

Even though the results for normal rein tension are correlated with outcomes of previous studies of Preuschoft (1995, 1999) and Clayton et al. (2003), the results for halt and punishment methods are strikingly different. Warren-Smith et al. (2006) reported that the tensions applied for the halt response were much greater than those required for any other response (up to 43 N) and that responses can be achieved with far lower tensions (9 N) than previously reported by Clayton et al. (2003) up to 60 N.

Our findings demonstrate that the halt is not the strongest aid that the rider is able to apply to horses' mouths. The tensions recorded in both reins when halting (with a mean of 137 N and maximum of 235 N) were significantly lower than the tensions in the reins during any of methods of punishment. Maximum rein tension registered while method 2 was applied: 1754N (179 kg) for both reins and 1475N (150.5 kg) per one rein and with a mean of 1002 and 1240.5 N.

With a rein tension corresponding to "riding in collection", measurements varied between 78 N (3 kg) (Rider #4) to 98 N (10 kg) (Rider #5), discrepancies probably were due to the conformation, age, physical abilities and habits of the person applying force.

There was a significant difference, which varies from 284 N (29 kg) to 1754 N (179 kg), with both methods of punishment. There was no consideration of rein tension before the punishment test. Participants were asked to hold the reins as they normally would in their everyday riding. It should be mentioned that all participants held the reins with constant tension, and rider # 4 had a lower tension throughout the tests. While this was probably due to lower physical abilities, she demonstrated a force of 392 N (40 kg) in punishment method #1 and 284 N (29 kg) force in punishment method # 2. It should be considered, that all applications were able to cause strong pain (Cook, 2003; Bennett, 2009).

There were some, although not significant, differences in the techniques demonstrated, as all riders have a specific pattern in producing rein tension that is connected to their riding style. It can be an extra pressure in one of the reins, or a way of using the reins in a specific moment (Ödberg and Bouissou, 1999). Although these differences can influence the experiment they are beyond the scope of this study.

Evidently, individual differences in the sensitivity of the rider's hands may account for some of the apparent discrepancies (Ödberg and Bouissou, 1999). Such differences in sensitivity may relate to the perception of how tightly an object must be held to prevent slippage (i.e., grip force), the surface texture of the object (Flanagan and Wing, 1997), and whether the object is static or dynamic (Flanagan, 1996).

The difference in rein tension between the left and right reins in our study was not significant, although it is obvious that in our study, the left hand applied lower tension than the right which correlates with findings of Weber (1978) and Warren-Smith (2006). In the test of punishment method #2, however, only one rein was held fixed and the other jerked back. Clayton (2007) reported that if the reins were used asymmetrically, the net effect would depend on the relative forces applied to the active and opposing reins. It was not possible to produce an independent effect on one side of the mouth (Clayton, 2007), so we summarized right and left rein application data to demonstrate general force applied to the horse's mouth.

It is important to note that the mannequin did not have the physical resistance of a living horse. Clayton (2003) found that rein tension related to the footfalls of the horse and the nodding of the horse's head. Any head movement of a live horse in an attempt to avoid bit-induced pain can influence the result of the force applied to its mouth (Cook, 2007a). At the same time, as rein tension increases, the elastic nature of the horse's lips results in a larger area of lip contacting the bit, while the tongue is pressed with greater force, and both diastemas up to the second premolars can be touched or impacted (Clayton, 1995; Warren, 2005).

There was the opinion that the extent to which the bit causes pain is most likely related to pressure exerted by rein tension – something inexperienced riders have little control over (Hall et al., 2008). Warren-Smith (2006) reported that the least experienced rider exerted the most rein tension. Our experiment demonstrated that riders of different qualifications have similar abilities for inflicting pain on the horse. It was found that age, physical condition, and experience of the rider couldn't be taken into consideration when the bit is used. The leverage system of the reins, and the design of the bit, enables everyone to achieve more than enough force to cause pain (Cook 2003; Bennett, 2006).

4.3. Discussion of Riders' Answers of Questions

All participants were given the results of the experiment and asked to fill out the questionnaire. All of them were amazed by the results, which demonstrated that the riders had no idea about the harm and pain they caused to the horse by using a bit. It correlated with findings of Clayton et al. (2003) who reported that the rider's perception of rein tension was significantly different from the tension data obtained.

It was confirmed via an interview with participants that all of them apply punishment methods one to 25 times during each training session or competition (Table 3). De Cartier d'Yves and Ödberg (2005) reported that judges' ratings of "lightness" of rein tension did not correlate with concurrent rein tension data. In our research, there was also evidence that judges do not pay attention to such types of punishment, and that using the bit as punishment does not lead to disqualification in equine sports.

Five of the participants of the experiment declared that they were taught to punish the horse with the methods demonstrated in the experiment by qualified FEI trainers, as well as in Riding Schools. None of the riders were aware of the methods s/he used, and only three of them considered the methods to be painful. Five of the six riders stated that, even though they cause pain to the horse, it is worth it for the sake of equine sport.

All participants considered that the pain (even after they were given the results) was possible for the horse to bear and there was nothing bad about inflicting pain on the horse.

All participants admitted that in stressful situations, the fear during training and competition gave them much more power and ability to punish with the bit. They also declared that they became angry when they are training. However, it is impossible to assess the power used by fearful or angry riders in laboratory conditions because the participants were not under stress. Three of the participants were unsure if they were always adequately punishing the horse for its behaviour.

An additional question, not recorded in table3 was asked when all participants indicated that they were not going to change their methods. The question was, "Why are you not going to change the methods you use now?" Participants answered that "the methods used are very effective"; "there are no other methods of training available"; "all high-level sportsmen do this and gain great results"; "they are methods approved by the FEI"; "the methods used are consistent with learning theory" and "everybody does it, why should I reject it?"

To summarize, jerks of the first and second types of punishment have been thoroughly tested (179 kg). These methods are frequently and widely used in professional and amateur equine sport. It was found that even if the jerk were ten times weaker than registered in the experiment, it would still inevitably cause severe pain (Cook, 2003; Preuschoft, 1999; Clayton et al, 2003; Warren–Smith, 2006) and can be considered as cruelty.

4.4. Critique of Experimental Protocol and Suggestions

At first glance, some aspects of the protocol might appear to be weak, but the presence of witnesses and laboratory conditions balance the experiment. In the hope that others will repeat such experiments, some suggestions can be made.

The tests used in this experiment included tests of two basic punishment methods, while in reality many variations on the methods and style of punishment are possible. A similar protocol could be applied to a larger number of equestrians for a longer period of time in laboratory and field conditions. To avoid bias it would help if riders were unaware of the experiment. This would guarantee that the participants behaved normally under normal conditions. Riders could be novices or professionals in any discipline at any level, such as jumping, driving, or barrel racing.

The experiment described used only one type of bit, which was the snaffle. This bit is considered to be mildest in the range of bits available (Clayton, 1985;

"Punishment" Impact on A Horse's Mouth by the "Snaffle Bit"...

165

Warren-Smith, 2006). It is known that mechanical restraints and stimulants may be used to increase the pressure that riders can apply (McGreevy, 2009). Cook (2005); McGreevy et al., (2009) reported that there is a strong tendency for riders to use stronger bits as the first approach to solving a problem. More severe bits cause much more pain in the case of rein tension (Clayton et al., 2003; Cook, 2005, Warren-Smith, 2006). Many researchers suggested that the potentially painful leverage in combination with harsh materials such as mechanical hackamores could break a horse's nose and/or jaw with surprisingly little effort from the rider (Jahiel, 2001). Therefore, experiments with different sorts of bits in combination with gadgets used should be carried out.

It should be considered that the experiment was carried out in laboratory conditions, which prevents riders from experiencing nervous and emotional responses to the horse's behaviour. These responses may aggravate the methods for punishing the horse with a bit.

Although there is a strong need to test the punishment methods during real training, the author considered it cruel.

Video and photo recording could assist in future research.

5. CONCLUSION

Two main methods of punishment applied by riders in the equestrian world were tested. Both of these methods make the horse suffer varying degrees of pain and cruelty. The results of this experiment correlate with studies of other researchers, who consider that in the interests of horse welfare, an objective measure; such as tensiometry in order to evaluate "contact" and "lightness" should be used extensively (Warren-Smith et al., 2007). Riders need to become aware of the rein tensions that they are applying to horses and work to decrease them (McGreevy, 2009).

Preliminary investigations set an important baseline for further work. Others are encouraged to repeat similar studies, and suggestions are made for improving the experimental design. The authors are of the opinion that punishment by the bit represents pain, cruelty, and health problems for horses. Humanism and scientific research are not in alignment with the cruelty that is demonstrated by training techniques commonly used in equine sport. Further study in regard to bits, whips and other aids used in equine sport should be carried out and brought to public attention with collaboration of scientists and media sources.

APPENDIX 4

THE FORCE OF POSSIBLE STRIKES BY A STANDARD WHIP WHICH IS USED AS A STANDARD MEANS OF INFLUENCE IN EQUESTRIAN SPORTS

ПРАВИТЕЛЬСТВО САНКТ-ПЕТЕРБУРГА
КОМИТЕТ ПО ЗДРАВООХРАНЕНИЮ
**САНКТ-ПЕТЕРБУРГСКОЕ
ГОСУДАРСТВЕННОЕ УЧРЕЖДЕНИЕ
ЗДРАВООХРАНЕНИЯ
«БЮРО СУДЕБНО-МЕДИЦИНСКОЙ
ЭКСПЕРТИЗЫ»**
195067, Санкт-Петербург,
Екатерининский пр., 10
тел. (7-812) 544-1717;факс (7-812) 545-0340
ОКПО 01932390 ОКОГУ 07185
E-mail: sudmed@zdrav.spb.ru

14.12.2006 г. № 366 /01-4

А К Т

испытаний по установлению силы возможных ударов
стандартным хлыстом, принятым в качестве штатного
средства воздействия в конном спорте,
и особенностей повреждений кожи и мягких тканей лошади,
возникающих в результате таких ударов

1. Цель испытаний: установление максимальной силы возможных ударов стандартным хлыстом, принятым в качестве штатного средства воздействия в конном спорте, а также особенностей повреждений кожи и мягких тканей лошади, возникающих в результате таких ударов.

2. Задачи испытаний:

– установление максимальной силы динамического воздействия стандартным хлыстом при ударах разными способами, с разной скоростью (от воздействия людей, обладающих разной физической силой), в разных направлениях по биологическим и небиологическим имитаторам, а также на специальном стенде;

– определение возможности образования повреждений кожи и мягких тканей лошади, возникающих в результате ударов разными частями стандартного хлыста с разной силой и скоростью.

3. Методика исследований и условия постановки экспериментов:

Экспертные исследования проводились согласно общей методике, применяемой в судебной медицине для медико-криминалистического изучения поражающего воздействия тупых предметов, а также механизмов огнестрельной и взрывной травмы (в том числе, так называемой «забронеовой травмы» тела человека, одетого в средства индивидуальной бронезащиты, например – бронежилет).

3.1. На первом этапе проводилось изучение и обобщение данных:

NEVZOROV HAUTE ÉCOLE
RESEARCH CENTRE
THE GOVERNMENT OF SAINT-PETERSBURG
HEALTH PROTECTION COMMITTEE
**THE STATE INSTITUTE
OF HEALTH PROTECTION
OF SAINT-PETERSBURG
"BUREAU OF FORENSIC SCIENCE"**
195067, Saint-Petersburg,
Ekaterininskiy pr. 10
tel. (7-812) 544-1717, fax. (7-812) 545 0340
OKPO 01932390 OKOGU 07185
E-mail: sudmed@zdray.spb.ru
14.12.2006 No 366 /01-4

STATEMENT

**of experiments to define the force of possible strikes by a standard whip,
which is used as a standard means of influence in equestrian sports,
and to determine the extent of damage to skin and soft tissues of a horse
that appear as a result of such strikes**

1. Purpose of examinations: determination of maximum force of possible strikes by a standard whip that is used as a standard means of influence in equestrian sports and to determine the extent of damage to skin and soft tissues of a horse that appear as a result of such strikes.

2. Experiments:

- definition of the maximum force of dynamic impact of a standard whip under strikes in different manners, with different speeds (by people possessing different physical strength), from different directions on biological and non-biological models, and also on a special stand.
- Determination of maximum force of dynamic influence by a standard whip while striking with it in different ways, with different speeds (from the influence of people possessing different physical abilities), in different directions at biological and non-biological models, as well as on a special stand.

3. Methods of analysis and conditions of setting of the experiments:

Analysis was carried out with coherence to general methods used in forensic science for crime-detection studies to identify the effects of a striking effect by blunt objects and also of mechanisms of bullet and explosive trauma (including "through the armor trauma" to the human body when wearing types of individual body-armor, i.e. a bulletproof vest).

3.1 The first stage included **studying and generalization of the data**:

a) Equine sport literature, photo and video materials from various competitions where riders were using an equine sports whip. Types of strikes and amplitudes of whip strikes accepted in equestrian sports, as well as possible force of given strikes were investigated.

b) Expert crime detection literature about the types and qualities of damages that appear:

— From the strike by hard blunt objects with limited traumatic surface applied with different amounts of energy (speed and force) on different biological objects;

— During blunt "through the armor trauma" to the human body, dressed in means of individual armor protection (protective vest, helmet and etc);

c) Materials from the archives of crime-detection records of damage done to victims who received trauma from a strike by a blunt object with a traumatic surface of small size, i.e. in conditions typical to those of strikes by a whip in equestrian sport;

d) Archival and video materials of veterinary studies of corpses of horses with welt marks from a whip used in equine sports;

As a result of the studies databases were gathered with differential-diagnostic tables.

3.2. As a means of influence, a standard mass-produced whip used in equestrian sports was used (one that had been used previously) with popper/flapper made of leather sewn lengthwise with thick thread in four rows of machine-sewn stitches.

3.3. For the application of strikes, people that that had different physical characteristics and different abilities to apply force were used.

3.4. The application of strikes, their force, types of strikes and amplitude of movement of hand with the whip were in coherence with variants of regular strikes, accepted within equestrian sport.

3.5. For objective verification of the force of given strikes by the whip measurement of this parameter on special measuring system for studying ballistics of trauma by blunt object to a subject behind a barrier were used.

3.6. Experiments were done on biological and non-biological models, analogical in its density to soft tissues of a living horse (blocks of ballistic plastic).

In order to define the exact boundaries of damage, as well as imitation of the zones of graze wounds on the skin the following method was used: in consecutive order blank sheets of writing paper and carbon paper (pigment side down) were placed on top of the objects to be struck.

4. Results of experiments were studied with detailed care (using standard methods of morphoscopy and morphometry), and were also recorded by photography using a digital camera.

As a result of studying the physical parameters of the striking effect of the popper/flapper of a whip used in equestrian sport with help of special experimental settings it was found that the general force of the whip was no less than 19 kg/cm^2 and the maximum energy of the strike was about 20–25 joule/cm^2.

During the following experimental studies it was found that as a result of strikes by a standard type of whip used in equestrian sport (with standard amplitude of strikes of this type) on a model of soft tissue of a horse, the following injuries were observed:

— On sheets of paper: deformation and trough ruptures of long oval form in size up to 6x1 cm with uneven, ruptured borders, surrounded with a zone of deposit of black pigment in width up to 0.5–1.0 cm (which follows the zone of a graze wound around the primary injury);

— On blocks of ballistic plastic impressions were formed, identical in form and size to the features of the striking surface of a mass-produced whip used in equestrian sport:

a) From strikes by flat surface – with total size of 9–10×2–3 cm;

b) From strikes by raised surface – 10–11×1.0–1.5 cm.

Damage on models of soft biological tissues like this usually coheres with the following types of injuries:

• Local injuries;
• Local bruises, subcutaneous hemorrhage and hematomas;
• Crushing of subcutaneous tissue;
• Detachment of skin at the place of traumatic contact;
• Ruptures of blood vessels;
• Lamellar hemorrhage under the muscle fascia;
• Multifocal and infiltrative hemorrhages into underlying muscles;
• Partial ruptures and crushing of muscles.

5. Results of the study of the materials from the forensic science archives of injuries of victims who were traumatized by being struck with a blunt object with a limited traumatic surface of small size, in conditions analogical to those experiments described above (those which are typical while giving strikes with the whip in equine sport) and also on biological models have shown that in cases like this, as a rule, following types of injuries were formed:

• Graze wounds;
• Hemorrhages and hematomas;
• Crushing of subcutaneous skin base;
• Skin detachment;
• Ruptures of blood-vessels;
• Hemorrhages into the fascia of muscle tissue;
• Ruptures and crushing of separate muscle fibers.

6. Results of the study of archival and video materials of veterinary necropsies of horses that had welt marks from the sport whip testify that in places of impact by the whip the following damages were discovered:

Graze wounds, hemorrhages and intradermal hemorrhages;

Crushing of subcutaneous tissue;

Hemorrhages under fascia of muscles;

Partial rupture and crushing of muscle tissue.

7. Comparison of obtained data.

7.1. All the data that has been described above, which was received as result of different studies and experiments was put together for comparison into Table 1.

Table 1.
Results of comparison of data by types of injuries

Main types of injuries	Generalization of special literature	Presence of injuries by results:			
		Archive materials		Experiments on models	
		Expertise	Veterinary	Biological	Non-biological
Graze wounds	+	+	+/–	+	+
Hemorrhages in:	+	+	+	+	+
– skin, intradermal	+	+	+/–	+	+
– the mass of subcutaneous tissue	+	+	+	+	+
– underlying muscles	+	+	+	+	+
Crushings of:	+	+	+	+	+
– the mass of subcutaneous tissue	+	+	+	+	+
– muscle fibers	+	+	+	+	+
– underlying organs	+	+/–	+/–	+/–	–
Ruptures of blood vessels	+	+	+/–	+	+/–

As a result of comparison of data in Table 1, it was determined that they are almost completely identical, this signifies the reliability of the data received regarding morphological signs that characterize the trauma caused by a previously used, mass-produced whip used in sport.

7.2. In the event of repeated strikes on the same area of the body, the size of injuries that were described above grows proportionately.

7.3. Aside from the local signs of the striking effect on the animal's body it is significant to note that frequent repeated hemorrhages and also crushing of tissue can cause general suffering of the organism.

These traumas are connected with a process of reabsorption of repeatedly induced hemorrhages (hematomas) and other tissue injuries.

During the process of reabsorption, cells are detached including hemocytes (erythrocytes) from the center of traumatized areas in the form of free protein – hemoglobin and myoglobin. These proteins and their debris, having a high molecular weight, have the ability to accumulate in small vessels (capillaries) as well as in the kidneys, obstructing them. Hemoglobin and myoglobin cylinders are formed, which can lead to nephrosis (an inflammatory disease of the kidneys).

All of this compromises the processes of filtration and discharge of waste products of metabolism, which cannot not affect in a negative way the health and general state of an animal.

SUMMARY

As a result of studies and experiments undertaken, it was identified that:

1. The general force of the striking effect of the popper/flapper of the whip used in sport is not less than 19 kg/cm^2 and the maximum energy of the strike is around 20–25 joule/cm^2.

2. Striking influences of given intensity may cause different injuries to biological tissues of an animal's body: from wounds, hemorrhages and to local crushing of subcutaneous tissue, rupture of blood-vessels and partial ruptures of underlying muscles.

3. Frequent multiple local signs of trauma by blunt object of soft tissue from striking effect of the whip on animals' body leading to hemorrhaging and crushing of underlying tissues can cause general suffering of the organism in general, including damage to the kidneys.

Medico-legal experts:

Deputy Chief of Bureau for Expertise
Doctor of Medical Science, Professor
Honored Inventor of Russian Federation
V. D. Isakov

Head of Corpse Expertise Department
Candidate of Medical Science
Doctor of Higher Qualification Category
V. E. Sysoev

Head of Nevzorov Haute École Research Centre
A. G. Nevzorov

www.ingramcontent.com/pod-product-compliance
Lightning Source LLC
Chambersburg PA
CBHW060926040426
42445CB00011B/818